DOUBLE TROUBLE

A Freedom from Social Oppression Anthology:
Creation of a Unique Sexual Identity

Michael Holloway King, M.D.

Author of

Hide and Play Dead:
From Memoir to Real-Time Healing

And

Overcoming Oppression:
Your Guide to a New Life

Contentment A Freedom from Social Oppression Anthology: Creation of a Unique Spiritual Identity is a work of non-fiction. Ideas have been given proper attribution and credit throughout the work. Any resemblance to other works is unintentional.

ISBN 1981251758

PREFACE

I am pleased to present the *second* of four anthologies, or collections of narrative pieces from my first book, "Hide and Play Dead." The organizing theme for this anthology is *sexual identity* or sexuality, which is a crucial part of the process of finding one's truest identity. Relationships are challenging for all persons, and yet love, and taking risks to find love, represents, perhaps, the greatest quest for meaning we share.

My experience of coming out and establishing a sexual identity was complicated by my internalized homophobia, bisexuality, and quasi-incestuous relationships with both my parents. My long series of ten foiled marriage-level relationships stems from my codependency—playing the role of a "house slave" who is easily exploited by narcissists and other difficult personality and emotional disorders. However, this collection strives to make my extremely challenging and convoluted relationship history as transparent as possible.

Although the reading here flows with the narrative, it cannot truly compare to reading the original text with all its segments and its format as a cohesive nonfiction novel—with building suspense, balancing light or metaphysical elements, and climactic pinnacles. Footnotes have been removed, and explanatory bridging sentences inserted instead, to preserve continuity to the subject of being gay.

You will also note that, due to my effort to heal my own post-traumatic stress disorder while writing the book, I include insightful "flashbacks" and bridging metaphors that may seem incongruent within this text, but would be easily understood in the book itself. However, they are full of innuendo and meaning in *any* format, whether in the original work or as discrete short stories.

The content here may be of great value for high school, college or university courses in several fields—especially Queer or LGBT studies, the social sciences, and English composition. I urge younger readers to suggest some of the following material to their professors or teachers, and for academicians to take a second look at what is revealed in these pages.

I also hope that readers will not only read the entirety of "Hide and Play Dead," but also my second book, "Overcoming Oppression." The subject of homophobia as a facet of prejudice is a central theme in "Overcoming Oppression," and, also, a vital issue of current social debate and extremist attitudes.

Feel free to visit my website and blog at: www.michaelhollowayking.com to leave comments or communicate with me directly through the blog pages, especially about the topics that this or my other works may pose. I also welcome writings from others to include in my blog and social media forums. My other anthologies center on the topics of *racial identity, adult identity,* and a metaphysical and inspirational anthology, focused on *spiritual identity.*

MICHAEL HOLLOWAY KING

ICE WALKING

Relationships are somewhat like walking on ice... There wasn't much for a child to do for adventure growing up in Erie, Pennsylvania, but one of my favorite pastimes as a child was to walk on a frozen pond in the early winter. Walking out onto a frozen body of water posed a certain danger, depending on how thin was the ice and how deep the body of water. My mother was always afraid that I might fall through a crack and drown under the ice barrier.

I would tentatively place my foot on the edge, to see if it cracked under light pressure. Usually, it did crack because the water was slightly warmer nearer land. Then, I used a stick to hammer the ice as far out as I could reach. That gave me an estimate of the inner edge. Then, I'd throw a rock farther out, to test the ice's strength in the middle of the pond.

None of these tests was really accurate, because my body weight was more than the impact of the stick or the rock. Nevertheless, it gave me a boost of courage to try walking out on my own. The edge would start to crack, so I had to slide quickly far out to the middle. Then I just stood there feeling proud.

When I was a teenager, I gravitated to the great lake, itself. Now the danger was very real. Even if one reached far out, there were unpredictable stretches of thin ice and I never knew where they might be and the lake was very deep. At some point, the ice cover disappeared completely because Lake Erie rarely froze its entire superficial veneer. But I never drowned and the adventure was worth the risk.

*

There was always a silver lining inside the umbrage of my clouds. Without healing relationships and positive experiences, I would have crumbled into hopeless depression early in life. That time will come *later*, but for now I am a lucky young man.

The best friend I *could* have had...

I'm just beginning to "come out" and explore the gay world in 1975. I notice a posting about a gay and lesbian dance at MIT. It sounds good, and far better than my failures at gay bars. I should meet a better pedigree of peers at MIT, although they might all be nerds.

I arrive and find a hundred students gathered in a noisy auditorium. Most of them are dancing and, unlike a dance in Erie a few years ago, I don't feel threatened. Oddly, it's fifty percent women. My homophobia is activated; for some reason, the presence of women makes it difficult to connect with a man. My fearful thought is that the women must be straight. They'll *judge* me. So, I act straight, at first.

I spot a woman standing alone, approach her, and ask her to dance with me. "OK, but just for a little while. I'm looking for another woman," she replies. "Perhaps, you'd be better off dancing with my boyfriend, Phillip—he's right over there." She points to an attractive blond fellow nearby.

Rita and Phillip are prototypes of a new age couple. They've been together since high school, and now Rita is in an accelerated medical school program at Boston University. Phillip is just "here," in love with her and not sure what to do in life. He's nineteen and had to leave home because his father became morbidly depressed after going bankrupt and ending up losing everything. So, Phillip is putting himself through college by working and taking out student loans.

Phillip is physically appealing and has long blonde hair. He is intelligent and very sweet. And he is straight. But this is Boston in the 1970s and straight men are "trying out" being gay. He feels abnormal to *not* feel sexually turned-on by other men, so he is trying hard to overcome his block.

I'm in bed with Phillip and Rita. Phillip is jealous when I start to make love to his girlfriend, so he pulls me gently off Rita and squeezes himself between her and me. Then he tries desperately to satisfy my sexual desire by himself. One afternoon when I am depressed, the couple comes over to my apartment to console me. Rita sits on the edge of my bed studying for an exam, while Phillip makes love to me.

For the next year, he would try to be gay for me, but our relationship remains a true, loving friendship. He looks up to me with an innocent respect and an open heart. Eventually, Phillip will marry a French woman and he will live a happy heterosexual life in France, adopting two lovely South American orphans. I miss Phillip terribly. He would have been the best friend I could have ever had…

Love has no limits.

*

The best marriage I *could* have had…

2

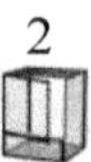

DOUBLE TROUBLE

It's 1980. I'm finishing my medical degree and about to embark on a future in international health. I'd never taken a course in art history at Harvard and I'd always regretted that. My parents are avid collectors of Asian art, and my inclination is toward Eastern philosophies and cultures.

One free afternoon I decide to check out the Fogg Art Gallery, the main art museum at Harvard University. There's a tour of Ming dynasty porcelain and the tour guide is a young professor of Asian art, the curator of the Japanese, Chinese, and Korean galleries.

Robert is a tall, articulate, and humorous fellow. My instinct tells me he's gay, too. After the tour, I make up some questions just to linger privately with Robert and there's a strong mutual attraction. We arrange to have a date at a Korean restaurant. I'm impressed as he orders a sumptuous feast, conversing with the cook in fluent Korean. Robert also speaks Japanese and two dialects of Chinese.

In all respects, Robert would be my perfect mate. But I'm foolish and young, about to venture abroad, and I don't like his somewhat high-pitched voice. It's the type of voice that may be useful when speaking tonal languages, but in English it sounds a bit effeminate and affected to me. I forgot that I, too, used to have a high-pitched voice as a child, and it was perhaps the only sign of my being gay. If I were to meet Robert today, the voice wouldn't matter at all. Back then, I was coping with my internalized homophobia and trying to be as macho as possible. I'd rehearsed my voice to make it sound deeper—with a lower tone and pitch—so that nobody would guess I was gay.

Robert grew up in the Midwest as the son of a wealthy rancher with high-level political connections. It was decided that the local public schools were not good enough for him, so the family hired a live-in Jesuit scholar to teach him one-on-one during the high school years. Robert turned out to be brilliant, but eccentric, having missed much of the usual adolescent socialization with a peer group. Feeling "different," he chose to find a home in the Peace Corps in Korea, then in Taiwan. He was like me—I also had to look abroad to find a sense of belonging.

I'm in the private, locked archives of the museum gallery and Robert is happily showing me priceless pottery and sculpture, explaining every detail about how it was made. I wander off a few yards, enthralled by the endless trophies of history. "Michael! Here— CATCH!" He tosses a Ming vase to me and I am terrified. Luckily, I catch it.

Robert laughs, and then he smiles beautifully at me. "That's the good thing about being a curator. You get to touch the art, to play with it, even to chip it to study its different layers. It's normal and OK to sometimes break something," he explains.

Robert is renowned in his field. When high-ranking officials from the Orient visit Harvard, he's asked to escort them around because he's so personable and linguistically gifted. As the world's #1 expert in jade and other art forms, he is often called upon to evaluate a wealthy family's private collection. He's used to rich people and doesn't like most of them. But one of the families that he *does* like is that of John D. Rockefeller III and his wife, at whose estate he often dines. When they decide to make their precious collection of Asian art available to the public, Robert becomes the curator for the Asia Society's impressive four-story headquarters on Park Avenue.

I visited Robert several times in New York and it was clear that he had fallen madly in love with me, but I was still ambivalent. Today I hate myself for missing an opportunity to be happy, and to be instead imprinted for abuse and compelled to seek out painful relationships that replayed my dysfunctional childhood. My fate took me away and astray, to the opposite side of the country, and Robert returned to Harvard from Park Avenue. We would correspond often, although less and less as the years passed by. Robert married a good fellow, an administrator at Harvard, and lives a contented life.

The last time I saw Robert was a few years ago when he came to San Francisco to consider being the curator of the new Asian art museum here; he could choose to be the curator at almost *any* museum, but he had become a true Harvardian at heart. We spent a night together in his hotel room. A week later, Robert sent me a beautiful card in which he wrote: *"The only regret that I have in life, the only thing missing, was that I failed to make you, Michael, my life's partner. I loved you, I still love you, and I will always love you dearly."*

Tears welled up inside as I wondered why I'd locked myself in the castle's turret. Why couldn't I have seen the knight who truly loved me down below? Why couldn't I have received the love and support that I craved?

*

Medical school signified a drastic derailment of my career aspirations that resulted in a loss of balance with my priorities weighted

4

too heavily on a desperate search for love and a skewed over-emphasis on relationships. I became compulsively addicted to having a partner, to provide a sense of identity and a purpose for my life. And I would fail at love because I would try to make it fill too big a hole in my life's process.

Each relationship was permeated with intense *shame* that matched the degree of my irresistible *attraction* to the partner. And each relationship harkened back to my earlier developmental history as I tried, unconsciously, to heal an aspect of my childhood wounds.

The subconscious thoughts were: *'If* I can make him or her love and support me, *then* I will heal my family history of abuse and trauma.' Or: *'If* I can make them like and accept and me, *then* I will be able to heal the sting of racism and social ostracization.'

The engulfing, or solipsistic, relationships I had with my depressed mother and my repressed father destined me to create a *finished* codependent identity— a house slave in the master's home, an eternal dependent child. I was programmed to reenact a desperate, needy approach to partners, vacillating between social predators and lessers.

I would find *fascinating and exotic partners*, all of whom would crush me under the yoke of narcissistic subjugation. Or I'd attach myself to a *popular group leader* to be sponsored into a desired peer group. But the quest always failed because figureheads do not want to usher others into the audience they possess. Conversely—since racial prejudice led to a feeling of intrinsic unworthiness—I'd rush to settle for less than I deserved. I would find *plain and ordinary partners* so I could fit in and not stand out. But that also failed; all of them were jealous of me and sought to further undermine my self-esteem.

All three types were capable of unspeakable acts of cruelty. I never fought back in self-defense. It was just my fate in life. I truly did love each partner, and they reciprocated love as best as a shame-based person could, although their instinct was to exploit me or withhold love instead.

What did I learn in each relationship? Did I learn something about spirituality or the nature of the world? Was this my strange way to finish a postgraduate training in psychopathology? What I *thought* I'd learn was based on fantasy, but I didn't care! I just wanted the experience of continually being in some relationship.

In this and the following chapters, I will relate the true stories of my ten live-together relationships, or marriages. The personages and events are real, although the names are fictitious. By some quirk of astronomical improbability, the ten people who I loved all suffered from what are called *Personality Disorders*. As a cluster, they represent a nearly complete compilation of the personality types that are most likely to be severely abusive, leading to trauma in those who attempt to love them. It is my hope that you will feel compassion for such persons. They are not responsible for their mental illnesses and they are still worthy of love.

My greatest life's lessons derive from long-term, committed relationships with all the most shame-inducing personality disorders, thereby gleaning first-hand knowledge that I am fortunate to now share with the reader. Many readers will have already been in a relationship such as one or more of these, whether it was with a family member, a co-worker, or an intimate partner and you will recall the lessons learned.

In my relationship history, all four elements of conditioning are stacked against my emotional recovery. Human minds are most imprinted by the *first*, the *longest*, the most *intense*, and the *last* of any given pattern. My first, my longest, and my most traumatic true loves were all narcissists, and the most recent involved psychopaths who threatened my life.

This memoir describes my first homosexual experience with my best friend in college— the nephew of the King of Morocco— and my homophobic return to the closet immediately afterwards. Leonard Bernstein is an important figure here. I am pleased to present this graphic and shocking narrative.

BEST FRIENDS

Jaimes and I become friends within my first week at Harvard College. I am exploring the freshman dorms to meet other classmates inside Harvard Yard. My "passport" is still the same and only one I know: *getting stoned together*. In complete contrast to Exeter, it's safe to indulge at Harvard College. Getting stoned or getting drunk is seemingly more than just OK; it's *endorsed* with libertarian nonchalance.

I roam about Harvard Yard and ring random buzzers of dorm rooms, offering to sell a gram of hashish to unknown classmates over the intercom. I don't care if they buy any. Some let me pass and we smoke and hang out together. But only *one* of them ever becomes more than an acquaintance; he turns out to be my best friend.

DOUBLE TROUBLE

Jaimes lives in a different kind of dorm outside of Harvard Yard that I found by sheer accident. It has more security and large, private rooms. We hit it off from the start. Jaimes is Moroccan, and smoking hashish is part of his cultural legacy. He's also warm and friendly toward me and we quickly find out that we have a lot in common, especially a similar sense of humor.

His English is fluent, as is his Arabic, French, German, and Italian. In fact, I soon lose count of how many languages he's learned and the many different countries in which he's lived—it's too confusing. We start to converse mostly in French because it is easy and fun for me.

Eventually, perhaps because we get stoned together and have an indescribable, mutual affinity, Jaimes confides that he is related to royalty and his uncle is the current King of Morocco. Anyway, I'd already asked him repeatedly why he had such a nice private room, and about all his fine things, his gold and silver and silk things. It doesn't matter if Jaimes is telling me the truth. It's as good an explanation as any for his special treatment in the college and why he speaks so many languages, especially Arabic.

One day when I visit Jaimes, he barely lets me into his room. When he opens the door, I notice he's sweating and panicky. *"Qu'est-ce qui se passe avec toi?"* I ask him, What's the matter ?

He points to an empty film container on the carpet in tremulous silence. "They're *spying* on me now. This is not mine. It's getting worse at home, much worse, I'm afraid."

Then, he tells me about what his uncle has done. There was an insurrection in Morocco and the King's enemies were captured. The King chose several of the leaders of the revolt to be televised "live" on national broadcasting. The King had them tied to posts and, one by one, he put a revolver to their heads and shot them "dead" for the whole nation to see.

I hold Jaimes while he trembles and console him with words, "You don't have to be so scared." The truth is that *I* am scared and *I* want to protect my best and only true friend from something unspeakably horrible.

Soon, Jaimes and I are hanging out together almost every day. He's eccentric and brilliant. When he's outside, he wears a Safari hat that looks ridiculous on him. But I never say that; he feels comfortable and at home in it. It's also bulletproof.

I continue to spend most of my *evenings* with Jaimes. There is an intimacy with him that kindles my intellect, my curiosity about the world, and more. We crack jokes in French and laugh together hilariously. We have both felt out-of-place since childhood, although for different reasons. We pass his gold pipe from lips to lips. I am finally comfortable because the ritual with Jaimes satisfies a bone-deep yearning that I cannot put into words or images.

I also have a girlfriend at Radcliff and I spend most of my *nighttimes* with her. I know I don't love her, but I can't imagine not having a girlfriend. Jaimes is solitary and spends his time in many venues. Sometimes, I see him with Marvin, another black student who will later end up being one of my classmates at Harvard Medical School.

Jaimes is a gifted musician and has decided to study opera. Unfortunately, I am not very interested in opera, and *fun* time together is truncated by his *rehearsing* time, which literally drives me away. I find out that I can't stand the sound of German opera. He is also teaching Arabic to graduate students—just for pleasure, certainly not for the money.

Then another intrusion comes into our time together. It's now my second year in college and I've moved to Quincy House and Jaimes has moved to Adams House. "Houses" at Harvard are clusters of fifty to a couple hundred students. They used to be fraternities; when the frat system was banned, the housing remained. Houses have a senior faculty member who carries the title, "Headmaster." It may be the chairperson of a department or a visiting scholar, but always a VIP.

Whoever gets the prestigious appointment as Headmaster also gets to live for free in a luxurious setting built inside the grounds of the House. Quincy House is a brick-and-gate enclosure of several vintage Ivy League buildings and one modern and impressive five-story structure. The Headmaster's residence is a four-thousand-square-foot penthouse with terraces and gardens atop the new building.

I will never be invited there, except for a few formal occasions like my graduation day. But Jaimes soon begins to go there, informally and often, starting in the second semester of our sophomore year. Sophomore year, second semester, and the new Headmaster of Quincy House is a visiting scholar—Leonard Bernstein. I'd often watched him on TV with my mother, conducting the New York Philharmonic. Mom was enthralled by Bernstein's genius and the show rekindled her never-fulfilled desire to become a concert pianist.

Jaimes moves into Quincy House exactly when Bernstein arrives. Students can't just change Houses like that; it breaks the "rules." In some way, I feel more than jealous. I need to know something that I *feel*, something far beyond the simple question that I ask the administrative secretary. I ask her why Jaimes gets a three-room suite just for him, while I must share a much smaller space with two roommates.

"I am not permitted to discuss certain matters, Mr. King. I'm sorry," she replies.

But at least Jaimes is two minutes away from my room now and we can spend more hours together, growing ever closer. Slowly, I begin to realize that Jaimes has some peculiar mannerisms, almost effeminate, and so does his friend Marvin. I'm just noticing things like this in other men.

I assume that it's an eccentricity of royalty, perhaps typical of the Moroccan court. It doesn't bother me when we are alone together. But I'm becoming embarrassed to be seen sitting with him in the public dining hall, especially when the black students glance over and stare at us. 'They're unaware of Jaimes' secret background,' I justify with rancor.

My two black roommates are the cruelest toward me. *Their* looks and whispers, sitting with the other black students in the dining hall, feel the most painful and dangerous of all. So, I sit with my girlfriend and ignore Jaimes. I realize that my public avoidance of my best friend, the nephew of the King of Morocco, is *mentally* crazy, but *emotionally* necessary. I arrange to sit with Jaimes in the special room for the French Club dinners twice a week; but listening to klutzes trying to speak French bores both of us.

Evenings in his room go unnoticed. My girlfriend asks me why I spend so much time with Jaimes instead of with her. "He's just a friend. I'm practicing French with him."

"How do you say 'I love you' in Arabic, Jaimes?"

"*Ana B hibbak,*" Jaimes answers. I begin to say the phrase to Jaimes often. It feels OK to say, "I love you," in a strange language that I don't know.

Gradually, I feel my odd and queasy jealousy growing and shifting and coalescing at deeper and deeper levels below my conscious mind. I stop *wondering* why Jaimes gets special treatment. I start *feeling* why. Then I start to feel *angry*. But I don't *know* exactly why.

Jaimes isn't in his room much any more. I start to knock on his door late at night, and then later and *later* and louder and *louder*—until I am pounding at his door. Then, I start to KICK his door. "JAIMES! If you're in there, let me in!" I shout. Suddenly, I must see him. *I must get inside!*

Until it is clear to me that he isn't sleeping in his suite most nights anymore. He'd just grin about it. Cloaked in mystery, again? I fear losing my best friend. I only push him away in *public*, but he is pushing me away in *private*. One night, I secretly follow him like a spy, and then I know: His music teacher is the Headmaster of Quincy House and Jaimes prefers to spend his nights *there* and not hanging out with me.

"Where do you *sleep* when you're with Bernstein?" I ask angrily. Somehow, I know more than I know. I desperately need something more than I can yet articulate. I'm becoming torn and jealous and crazy and confused. My anger now seems uncontrollable and completely irrational.

I *refuse* to see the image. I can't *imagine* the implications of such an image. I know *nothing* about "gay" or Bernstein. 'Sex with another man is not possible! It doesn't exist! *Do not expose this to me!* I cry out to the voice in my mind. I can't understand it. I simply will not get it.

In the late spring of my second semester, just before my 19th birthday, the instinct within my heart, my soul, and my groin finally erupts into my mind as a conscious concept and an actionable possibility. I knock at Jaime's door, frantically praying that he'll be inside. He is.

"Do you want to get stoned with me, Jaimes?" But I know the answer: He must protect his voice for the opera lessons. I gag and struggle with my tongue and breath to splutter out the *next* question: "Do you want to *have sex* with me, Jaimes?"

He's silent and just looks at me like he always has, without any surprise. Then he smiles and I sense an unspoken 'Yes.' I begin to take off my clothes, leaving my underpants on, which scarcely conceal my desire. I gently tug Jaimes' arm in the direction of his bedroom. He gets up from the gold-embroidered cushion on which he is sitting. My pent-up passion bursts in successive gushes without any pause for many hours. I am intoxicated with Jaimes' smooth brown skin, his trim muscular body, his full lips, and his masculine aroma.

In the morning, I speak my parting words to Jaimes in Arabic, "I love you, Jaimes."

"*Ana kaman babbak,*" he replies. *"I love you, too."*

I've had a breakthrough experience. But then, an iron curtain of excruciating guilt and shame clamps down on my soul and my genitals and shatters the pact. I never spoke to Jaimes again. For the next two years, I could not even look at Jaimes. After graduation, the Harvard Alumni Office listed his address as a PO Box at the United Nations. I never wrote to Jaimes.

Marvin, Jaimes' second best friend, died from AIDS in the early 1980s.

This memoir describes my 21st birthday in Paris, and an experience that lead to the fragmentation of my early gay identity.

LAST TANGO

I've arrived in Paris for my last summer of freedom before starting Harvard Medical School in the fall. My parents hesitantly granted my wish to have one last chance to study languages before giving it up to study only medicine. I promised I wouldn't spend much money; I'd live frugally, in the cheapest hotels or whatever I could find for nearly free.

I am a roving, roaming camel running loose without its rider but still carrying the cargo: my backpack and two enormous suitcases filled with language books and dictionaries for Spanish, French, Italian, Portuguese, and German.

Le Gai Paris! It's June and fragrant and wild. Today is a very special day: It's my 21st birthday.

The last four weeks in Boston, I'd studied something *different* from languages. I came to realize that I was probably gay and that I was not alone. A friend from Erie who was living in Boston told me that his new roommate was openly gay. I arranged for an introduction. "Bob" was the gay fellow's name. I had a secret agenda; a note in my hand would carry a message to Bob like a letter in a bottle, an entreaty for rescue. It said: 'I think I'm gay. Can you help me?'

I didn't care what Bob looked like or acted like, I just needed help. It had been almost two years since my experience with Jaimes and I was desperate for contact. When I tried to slip the note into Bob's parting handshake, it fell from his open palm to the sidewalk. To my disgrace and horror, he picked it up and read it out loud in front of my friend from Erie. But Bob did call me and we met in private. He taught me about gay sex and gay men. And he warned me to be *very* careful.

I've just gotten off the Metro and entered the West Bank of the Seine, the Latin Quarter—the bohemian, *artsy craftsy* area. I see a tall young black man trying to sell his art craft to passersby. He notices me and beckons me to come. I walk to him, like I once walked to a strange boy in an alley when I was four years old.

His name is René, he's from Martinique, and he's been living in Paris for ten years now. He is beautiful and muscular and has smooth, ebony skin, like Jaimes had, or Cullen, my father's handyman long ago. But his demeanor is super-macho and strange. His art of African motifs is mediocre. He persuades me to hang out with him. "Maybe you can help me get some American girls to buy my art?"

I notice that René doesn't just let "No, merci" simply pass. He gets loud and belligerent with stubborn buyers. After a while, he packs up his wares and invites me to go see a movie with him. A woman in front of us on the theater's escalator responds to something René says behind her back by turning around and spitting on him. "She's just racist!" he explains.

Serendipitously I run into three classmates who have also just graduated from Harvard! 'It must be a synchronistic sign of good tidings on my birthday,' I think. Good? On a deeper level, I feel I need some people to protect me, but why?

We all decide to celebrate my 21st birthday in the glorious Parc Montsouris□. My troupe collects food and wine, and René offers to be our guide. Soon the sun is setting and René asks me where I'm staying. "In a pension," I answer. He insists on knowing how much I'm paying and declares it's too much. Then, he invites me to stay with him for free at his apartment in the outskirts of Paris. Why not? I'll save money.

René doesn't pay for the Metro ticket; he dodges under the turn-style and orders me to do the same. I hesitate; why not just pay? He gets angry and yells something insulting that I don't understand. I follow his order, looking back at the ticket booth where a man is pounding on the window and shouting at us.

Two young women are sitting facing us on the high-speed train to the *faubourgs,* the extensive ring of suburbs around Paris. René speaks to them. They look startled. Again, he says something that is too crude for me to understand. But the message is clear: One of the women slaps him, and then they both move to other seats. I am getting scared as the Paris city lights recede into the distance. I'm lost somewhere in the *faubourgs* and I sense I'm being lead into the lair of a possible predator who insults women who spit on him and slap him. 'What could be the harm if I hang low, for just one night? Besides, he is beautiful, but no way *gay,*' I muse.

It's after midnight when we arrive at René's apartment. It's a cramped single room in a dilapidated tenement house. It has a musty, dank smell and poor lighting. There's a double bed and wood crates for furniture. It's incredibly hot inside. The toilet is down a long rickety hall. René undresses completely and I leave on my underwear.

I'm lying face up next to him when I sense his energy. I feel irresistibly drawn to him and I want to feel his hard body just once. I decide to hug him. He takes my hand down to his groin where his mast is fully erect and massive. "I know what you want!" he growls in French.

Suddenly, he forces me face down on the bed. "No, René, I just wanted to hug you. It's OK. I'm sorry!" I mutter. He spits on his hand to lubricate his cock. I'm terrified; I feel weak, breathless, and helpless. *What is he going to do?*

His strength overpowers me as he plasters me down. His stranglehold and weight on my back are crushing the air out of my lungs. Then, he penetrates me without warning, thrusting a hot iron that pierces my virgin anus. The pain is unbearable and I start to cry. "STOP!" I beg. He pinions me even harder; the pounding inside rips my tissues. I am biting a pillow and clutching the bars of the headboard as hard as I can to displace the pain. Finally, he moans and weakens; he has finished with me.

I shove him off and run down a corridor to the toilet stall that I will also see in nightmares for the rest of my life. I bolt shut the door's flimsy lock and brace it with my legs. I see blood dripping into the basin. I am on a wooden toilet seat like a toddler where I will stay all night, crying, even when René knocks angrily on the stall's door and orders me to come back to bed.

In the morning, I will escape on a train to Italy. I have never returned to Paris since the night of my 21st birthday. Another lifelong slave pattern has been stamped and branded on my body, my identity and my brain. A primordial distrust of others has taken root, and I no longer trust the process of my life's unfolding.

This is the first of ten "marriage memoirs," which depicts my marriage to a future Hollywood star—starting as a child star that grew into the epitome of narcissistic shallowness. It overlaps with the ending of my sexual ambivalence and establishing a gay identity.

I had no concept of homosexuality, only *homoeroticism*, as a child. Sometimes, I crossed my legs like my mother, thigh on thigh, and noticed that others raised their eyebrows. So, I crossed them ankle-on-thigh instead. Although keenly attuned to my mother, I was not clingy

or over-protected like the prototypical "Mama's boy" and I was not perceived as effeminate. My voice remained high-pitched until late adolescence, but I was not bothered about it until much later, when I could not talk over the loudspeakers to women, and then men, at dances or bars.

Exeter was the birthplace of an instinct for human bonding that would break part of the dam of self-suppression, where drugs were only a prelude and a passport to that new pillar of my identity as being gay.

My internalized homophobia, feeling intensely ashamed about my sexuality, began only a year before my first gay sexual experience with Jaimes. I was suddenly embarrassed by my first tenor voice and practiced forcing it to be lower. I wore cologne, cowboy boots, and cowhide vests because I couldn't imagine a gay cowboy. I deliberately acted masculine to the utmost detail, albeit with a hint of gentleness and sentimentality forbidden to most macho men.

But this initial shame about acting in congruence with my homosexual impulses lasted only a few years. I soon grew extremely proud of being gay in the 70's "liberation movement," although I would always appear straight to others and prefer to associate with masculine-acting men for the rest of my life. As an openly gay man, I felt the pride of a gypsy or a pioneer. Determination, courage, and a new self-confidence had now surfaced as I told my friends, teachers and relatives, "I'M GAY!"

Comfortability with my sexual orientation opened doors to an untapped love reservoir. I was enveloped and enraptured by love, giving it to others with abandonment of my Self. I had already been taught the virtues of self-abnegation and self-sacrifice—to serve all my partners "like a slave."

But I had to learn a life's lesson the hard way. The more I made myself a subservient object and suppressed my individuation, the more exploitative my partners would become. It is almost like the law of "supply and demand"; such a high supply of giving cheapened the worth of my altruism. And it was an exact reproduction of what I did for my mother, and she had done for her father, and so on....

I continued to search for true love, for a special partner, and for a supportive peer group. I still longed for love for, without it, a lingering nagging loneliness haunts me. I'd never had nurturance from a stable maternal bond or guidance from a physically available father figure. I'd never had true playmates or friendships with peers to offer validation and acceptance. And I'd never had co-visionaries or soulmates to encourage me to fulfill my destiny.

*

THE DIVA
My 1ˢᵗ marriage…

It is late spring of my second year in medical school. I'm twenty-two and I'm still sexually confused. A few months ago, I drove to Wellesley, the sister school of Radcliff, to attend a small black dance party in search of a girlfriend. That cold autumn night, I saw the woman of my dreams: Julia stood out from among all the others. But she was well protected inside her coterie of close friends. She was not going to be an easy catch and she knew it.

Julia was tall, stunningly beautiful, and *slender*. She had reddish-blond hair down to her shoulders, a cream-colored complexion, and genuine laughter. I approached her nervously and asked her to dance with me. Julia had studied ballet and I was not a good dancer. She joked about my awkwardness and tried to teach me some steps.

I had to have her. I needed to know that I was worthy of the best woman because, semi-consciously, I knew my true inclinations were elsewhere.

But there was one *last task* I had to accomplish before I could…

Julia embraces feminism with a red banner. One day, she is lying beside me at the beach studying. Then she starts slapping me with her shoes accusing me of "Chinese foot binding." She also has racial issues about being "just too white-looking" and having cousins who decided to give up trying to be black altogether. And she doesn't like my smoking pot or slipping sardines into her bubble bath water. Once, she even tried to strangle me and threw my bag of marijuana over the balcony of my twelfth-floor apartment into the pool below.

My parents approved highly of her and we got engaged.

Now, I felt that I could…

The gay scene in Boston is awful for me. The bars are racist, and I am timid and young. I just stand in a corner, hoping that somebody, *anybody*, would approach me, or that I could muster the courage to approach somebody by myself. I'd maybe walk over to a straggler after "last call," when only a couple of guys are left inside and the music stops playing.

I've even stooped to being dragged to the apartment of a hideous transvestite who called me his "prince." He telephoned people to wake them up and brag about catching me, while I sat disgusted on the edge of his bed. I ran away after giving him a false phone number.

*

Allani is tall, stunningly handsome, and *sleek*. He has dark brown hair down to his shoulders and a slightly tanned complexion. But his laughter is different from Julia's; it seems rehearsed. I approach him nervously in the bar and ask him to chat with me.

Allani keeps scanning around, as if to see who is looking at him or to find someone more worthy of his attention than me. Then he seems to look at me, or through me, but not *see* me. He does not reciprocate my interest, but we still end up going back to his apartment together. Then he doesn't reciprocate my interest again.

I feel as unworthy of Allani as I feel unworthy of Julia. I decide that I must offer Allani something to *entice* him to want me. I offer to relinquish my engagement with Julia. Julia tells me, "You have to decide, Michael. If you choose to be with him, I will never speak to you again." I have not heard a word about Julia or from Julia since 1976. And I never succeeded to make Allani love me.

Allani is a racial hybrid and is almost my color. He grew up in Hawaii and he's Hawaiian, Portuguese, and Chinese. But he is completely at ease with the ambiguity. Somehow I dream that Allani will bridge me across the racial divide and heal my racial wounds. He tells me that when race riots broke out at his high school in Los Angeles, the blacks and the whites each asked him which group he belonged to. "Neither!" he proudly declared.

Allani is a boastful talker. He claims to be a direct descendent of the last queen of the Hawaiian Islands. His family is suing for the usurpation of beachfront property worth untold millions. He'd moved to Los Angeles and was the youngest actor in the LA Civic Theater, playing Bernardo, the leader of the Sharks in "West Side Story." Then he'd moved to Tahoe and worked as a highly paid blackjack dealer, even though he was underage. The management let it slide because he was so clever, he says. Now he's a jazz vocalist enrolled at the prestigious Berklee College of Music and told me that he is the only student to have ever given a personal concert there.

But what he talks about most is being Don Ho's "child star" who sang on stage in huge concert halls full of tourists. It seems that he is fixated at the age of four to maybe nine years old: a beautiful, exotic, bronze-skinned child whose parents were well paid for his daily performances. He'd grown used to applause and adoration as a child star, like Michael Jackson, with whom he would later become "best friends." It seems that Allani's whole body is frozen as that of a child: a hairless, sunken chest, an innocent, bright-eyed face, and he's even a bit clumsy when not doing dance rehearsals.

A child star…age three to seven…excessive admiration that is never balanced with realistic feedback…being praised for perceived exceptional looks and talents by adults…

I just didn't know, back then.

Allani has grand expectations, *great* aspirations, and he is driven toward fame like a bolt of lightning into a metal rod. He knows lots of rich and famous people. I financially support Allani during the three years of my first live-together relationship. In return, I am swept off my feet into the dizzy world of the stage where Allani's ego is protected behind an impenetrable wall of smug arrogance.

His role is always to be the star, and *my* role is to exist as a tag-along member of his audience. *His* world is a gilded glittering world of sparkles and bubbles I've never imagined. Thanks to Allani, *my* world during medical school is something my classmates could never experience: drama.

I rush to the door to greet the young Italian countess who is one of Allani's many "best friends." He has lots of friends, depending on the relative current market value they have. I know that the lady's father is a past president of the American Bar Association and I've been told that she has acted in some Fellini films. The countess lives in a replica of the Carcassonne Palace, constructed on the north coast of Boston. Allani had shown it to me, to gawk at before meeting her, so that I'd be prepared. But I am *not* prepared for the bulimic beauty at the door. The countess is a scantily dressed mademoiselle wearing very high heels. She has two nasty, growling poodles on her shoulders, balanced on her mink stole.

"Where's *ALLANI!*" she demands as she imperiously pushes her way into my living room without even saying "Hello." She drops the dogs down to sniff the piano. As usual, Allani must make a grand entrance and *my* line is to say, "He's getting ready!"

The countess sighs loudly, shrugs her shoulders, and shakes her long hair in annoyance. I suggest we three go to the Isabella Stewart

Gardner Museum, without the poodles. It's the grandest public exhibit of coveted wealth I know. We walk three astride through the palatial halls of the four-story mansion filled with fabulous artwork that all used to belong to a "famously deceased" neurotic woman.

The countess is in the middle holding both our hands tightly. She saunters in her high heels and mink stole whose head and tail drape down her low-cut neckline, toward bra-less breasts that burst half exposed just above the nipples. We pass between two museum guards who stare, mouths agape at us. The countess immediately jerks Allani's hand and mine, to squeeze our palms hard onto her breasts. "I like to *SHOCK* people!" she says, as she laughs haughtily and shakes her long hair again.

I witness the thrill of Allani's performances with his jazz group. I admire his portfolio portraits that he got for free from an artist who is in love with him, like everybody, of which *all* are in love with him. He autographs two enlarged photos, which are extras that he doesn't want, for me to keep as souvenirs. One day he even lets me touch some knobs in a recording studio, to pretend to mix the music like my father had once briefly let me hold the string of a kite.

I witness the thrill of Allani's home theater that never stops. Dance troupes rehearse for hours in our home. Allani leads the group of women dancers, all having a crush on Allani, all wanting Allani, all pounding their feet, back and forth, the full length of the upper floor of our South End apartment. The apartment has Venetian-sculpted marble fireplaces and real crystal chandeliers. It was once a wealthy neighborhood, but then became a ghetto for Beatniks and blacks. At least it looks good, superficially.

Allani needs a stage and I'd do anything to help my partner. I decorate and furnish the apartment and cover the living expenses and do the housekeeping, all during my "spare time" in medical school. I take a semester off from school to work at UPS as a truck loader and make extra money to pay for our modestly showy lifestyle. I surrender myself completely to my first true love, slavishly seeking his love in return. Allani never says that he appreciates my contributions.

But one day he teaches me something very precious. It's at a Portuguese festival on the Boston beachfront. Allani and I are walking side-by-side, shirtless, in short shorts and getting attention—*lots* of attention. People are staring at us as we stroll past the booths. Allani likes it. I feel embarrassed. "Why are they looking at us, Allani? Is it because of our *skin color?* Do we look *gay?*" I fret.

"No, Michael. It's because we're *beautiful!*" That one comment changed my life. Every relationship offers a jewel of awareness; it was the first time that stares could, just possibly, mean something positive about me.

*

Another comment changed my life soon afterwards. My mother calls me. She and Dad have recently returned from travels in the Orient. Mom is very distraught as she asks my opinion about Dad's "strange" behavior on the flight home. "I had the window seat, as usual, and your father was in the middle and a man that we don't know had the aisle seat. Well, your father was talking with that man and then they were holding hands!"

She pauses and seems to choke on the next sentence. "Then, the man went to the toilet and…*your father went inside with him.* They were in there for a long time. Your father said he had to do some sort of medical exam. Michael, I'm frightened. He leaves me so many nights to deliver babies. I call the hospital and he's not there. Then, all his golfing buddies, but he's not at the golf club. What's going on?"

I see the whole picture in a flash. The events, the looks, and the innuendoes suddenly make sense. *Now*, I feel I could also… "Well, Mom, maybe he's *bisexual.* Lots of people are, you know. In fact, *I'm bisexual*, and I'm living with a great guy who I love."

My father calls me on his office phone shortly afterwards and is livid. "Don't ever, *ever*, come to my defense again! You don't know how much trouble you've caused, Michael!" Allani is furious, too. He's been indirectly outed, and now my parents pose a risk. He is determined to stay *in* his closet, because *outside* might interfere with his career aspirations.

I tell Allani about my problems in med school; Allani tells me to just be like him and get over it. *He* doesn't have any problems, only frustrations about inferior people who refuse to give him the recognition he deserves. Somehow he makes me feel lucky to get to be his audience and to hold him in bed, although he sleeps with his back turned toward me and pushes me away.

I also get used to Allani ignoring me with disdain when others are present. He can't include me in his conversations with more important people and he doesn't want anybody to even *think* we have a relationship. I'd have to become much more important before he'd care about me. I can't let myself know that I am only a marginal part of Allani's plans, serving as his "vehicle." I fantasize that I would become an otolaryngologist, an Ear-Nose-and-Throat specialist, so that I could take care of Allani's vocal cords and become his personal physician for the rest of my life, *without recognizing…*

Allani gets a phone call from Hawaii, from his "ex" who is serving prison time for some crime. Allani changes to a Hawaiian dialect to prevent me from understanding the words, but I understand the content. Finally, I realize that I am not who he wants to be with. I am just a steppingstone to the next level.

After three years of living together, I sadly close the apartment and go off to do a medical externship in rural Colombia for several months. Then, I return to Boston after working in the jungle to see Allani and try to reconnect. I still want him, even though he's not written or called me for the nearly four months apart. He reluctantly opens the door of his new apartment with a brusque coldness. He refuses to hug me or even touch me, and scarcely allows me to sleep on the floor at the foot of the bed like a dog. It's the same bed I'd bought that used to be *our* bed, but now it's in *his* new apartment, which is filled with my furniture and my stereo equipment—all that he'd taken from me because he "needs it."

He has cut his hair short. He's trying to look butch and stylish for stardom. "You're a hazard to my career, Michael. It's *over.*" I cried for the next three months. My life was *over.* Then I realized that the only Allani there was to love was Allani's picture in the portfolio or Allani live on stage. He could receive love *only* in the form of adulation and *only* when performing. There was no deeper Self inside to receive any offering of love at all. The only Allani that existed was the actor *it*-self.

Allani moved to Las Vegas and became the lead male accompanist with Diana Ross. Then he moved to Hollywood and opened a recording studio. I tracked him down for a last phone call. He boasted about his concert tours through Europe, he boasted of Michael Jackson and Prince and Madonna and Sammy Davis, Jr. and whoever is "Who's Who" in Hollywood. He knew them all, every detail about them. If they were famous, they were his "best friends." Allani had lots of "best friends." I saw him on MTV and turned it off.

This second marriage represents the international black struggle against racism, along with elements of high-profile politics and Marxism. It depicts a Paranoid Personality

Disorder— within the Latin American cultural context of machismo.

MACHO MAN
My 2ⁿᵈ marriage…

It's 1979 and I'm in my last year of medical school. I'm finally allowed to take electives—a free range of courses and environments, as per one's eclectic interests in medicine. Most students at Harvard Medical School will take rotations in advanced gastroenterology, research assistantships in endocrinology or cardiovascular surgery, and the like.

I choose to leave Boston and roam far, far away.

And my life will be topsy-turvy and chaotic for the next two years.

I'm in Medellín, Colombia and I have two weeks before I'm expected at the jungle hospital in remote Apartadó, a city *en route* to General Noriega's Panama. Strolling the evening streets of Medellín, I spot a blond man who is conspicuously both gringo and gay. A handsome swarthy fellow with a macho aura walks confidently astride him. The tough, macho guy is one hundred percent Colombian, a Socialist-Marxist Afro-Colombian historian, and most definitely, "my type."

I'm feeling insecure, as well as sensing that I need protection in a foreign land, especially as I am about to engage an unknown and somewhat risky assignment. So, paradoxical logic says that I must approach a potential abuser, a "Mr. Tough Guy," for protection from abuse…

Roberto comes from a proud family lineage, a very proud lineage and a tragic lineage. His mother is white and grew up in Madrid before her family moved to Bogotá. His father is, or was, of pure African ancestry and grew up inside the sultry archipelago of the western coast of Colombia. He is a direct descendent of the fugitive slaves who escaped the death colonies of the fortress at Cartagena, called *cimarrones*.

They formed strong free black African towns, or palenques, dating back to the 17ᵗʰ and 18ᵗʰ centuries. Nineteenth-century Colombians mapped a racial hierarchy onto national regions, and assigned technology and modernization to states that they marked as "white." Places marked as "black" or "Indian" were intentionally left in disorder, backwardness, and danger.

I said Roberto's father was, because he is dead. He was a self-made success story, a man who defied racism and rose to preeminence in the Capitol. He became a top graduate of the Colombian equivalent of Harvard Law School, a Supreme Court judge, then the "Chief of the Border" —the Aduanero General de Bogotá. He was responsible for all international trade and the supervisor of customs, imports, and exports. In 1979, that title meant one thing above all others: full knowledge and responsibility for the worldwide drug market, the trafficking of cocaine, and the emerging stranglehold strongholds of the Medellín and Cali drug cartels.

Roberto's father killed himself. That was probably better than the alternative in such circumstances. It protected his family from unspeakable danger. It protected his honor, because there is no pride like that of a black Colombian man who rose high up from the swampy ghettoes of oppression. It protected his integrity, for he was the national captain of law and order and justice, with an unflinching, staunch morality, and he did the honorable deed of sinking onboard the ship called "Colombia." Roberto's father was slated to run for the presidency when he committed suicide.

The pride and arrogance of the rebellious field slaves of Colombia carried forwards, as Roberto's father was the "first and only" black to reach the highest academic and political levels in the nation. And so did the merciless pressure to prove oneself academically superior to whites, as the subset of rebels comprising the black intelligentsia. But the status of climbing the social ladder did not pass on to his son.

"My grandfather placed outrageous expectations on my mother from an early age."

Roberto was the first-born and, as a son, he was expected to carry the baton of achievement forwards. But he balked and dropped out of his father's alma mater law school. Roberto rebelled against the brutal physical and emotional force that his father heaped upon him to make him to achieve notoriety. He took a hacksaw to the social ladder and declared his own freedom, like that of the *cimarrones* centuries before.

"Roy, Jr. was simply being given a crafted destiny passed down over the course of generations: The rebellious field slave who, upon Emancipation, rose to the top of Academia."

Roberto is a consummate intellectual and a radical left-wing historian. He is one of the first scholars to document the African

Diaspora in Colombia. He is also an underpaid teacher and a perpetual student. His family name and fame make him a big fish in the smaller lake of Cali, Colombia, where we would set up our home and try to build a life together. Roberto Augusto will become "Rob" and he will struggle to pronounce "Michael." So, I will become Miguelito and sometimes he'll call me Narciso, which means "Narcissus." All Americans are capitalist invaders, so all are generic narcissists in Roberto's mind. And, besides, Roberto likes to tease me, when he's not arguing with me instead.

I'm in the regional hospital in the middle of banana plantations carved out of dense jungle. Lusty and romantic love letters from Roberto arrive every few days. I'm touched by his devotion; we only spent ten days together in Medellín. After I leave the jungle, Roberto snatches me up and wants to show me the northern coast of the country—at my expense, of course, because he's "just a poor student."

We're touring the massive stone fortress of Cartagena, and he is openly and boldly affectionate toward me. Yet he is also blustering and macho, correcting and arguing with the female tour guide. The guide speaks only Spanish, since there is little need for English or other languages. Tourists don't usually come to see the legendary slave capitol of history.

"It is estimated that half a million slaves were used to build the fortress and their life expectancy was only three years. When they could not work anymore, they were thrown into these crocodile pits for amusement. A few managed to escape as *cimarrones,*" the guide informs the audience. She nonchalantly waves her hand toward some long empty concrete vats. My imagination sees a vivid series of horrible and gruesome images.

The word given these notorious and historic rebel slaves, *cimarrones,* also means "wild Mustangs" in Spanish. They recreated their tribal culture in relative freedom, protected by the Andes Mountains, vast waterways and swamplands, hiding where almost none could find them. Transportation between the islands was by canoe. Communication across the islands, necessary to send the alert of Spaniards searching for their missing slaves, took the form of yodeling tones that traveled across miles, which then became a form of incantation, and then a wonderful music.

We're on the hot beach in Cartagena. You can rent private tents here, which is great if you're gay. Inside the tent, Roberto tells me about how his father would beat him, yell at him to "achieve," and when Roberto dropped out of the Harvard-equivalent law school, his father cut off all financial support and refused to talk to him. I sense the parallels between his slave ancestry and my own, yet in a different country with a different history.

I fumble for the words to say, "I have a lot of compassion for you." But there is no clear translation for that in Spanish, and the word "compassion" also has a nuance of meaning "pity." Roberto snaps into a rage, insulted! How dare I pity him? He insists that I knew exactly what I'd said. Roberto is my hot-tempered, rebellious, macho Latin lover. I excuse him for the temper, because one must respect the cultural context of acquired behavior. Aren't all Latin men hot-tempered, rebellious, and macho?

It's my first night back in Colombia, reunited with Roberto after five months back in the States, working on the Zuni Indian reservation. I'm in an open, outdoor concert arena. There are ten thousand people gathered here to listen to Leonora González Mina, the "Great Negress of Colombia" —the most renowned black singer of Latin America, who has kept alive the traditional yodeling music of the *cimarrones*. La Negra Grande de Colombia is also Roberto's aunt and we will visit her house freely. She wants to send her son to the Berklee College of Music in Boston and asks me if I know about it. It hurts to be reminded of Allani. She agrees to co-sign the lease for the little house I will rent to live in with Roberto as my domestic partner.

Roberto looks like me to the point of passing as cousins. That makes him happy; being in the quasi-closet, when it's politically advantageous to do so, is easy when you live with somebody who looks like you. He tells people that I am his "American cousin" and no embarrassing questions are asked. Roberto has connections to a woodcrafter who designs handmade wood and leather furniture to fill the two-bedroom bungalow. He has lots of connections, whereas I know nobody here. I am becoming increasingly dependent on Roberto to teach me the rules, keep me safe, and introduce friends to me.

We're at Silvia's ranch in the countryside outside of Cali. It's the usual "Sunday afternoon extended family gathering" with Silvia, her three beautiful children, and her two homely sisters. There are toasts with aguardiente, the local equivalent of whisky, and sumptuous dining on her incredible shellfish sancochos and exotic smoothies. There will be rounds of stories and jokes, tears and laughter that go on for many leisurely hours.

Silvia is also Afro-Colombian. She's a social worker. She's middle-aged and she's divorced. She likes me, but she secretly loves Roberto.

And she has a fantasy. We're at home and Silvia wants a three-way. Roberto is eager.

As we start, the doorbell rings…

It's a beautiful tall black man, a student of Roberto's, who Roberto tells, "We're having an orgy, like to join?"

The stranger is now on top of Roberto, but Roberto is a "top" and is protesting, while I'm fucking Silvia. I'm jealous of Roberto and want to seduce the fourth intruder for myself, away from Roberto, so I join the two men. Silvia gets angry because I've interrupted coitus, and then she's crying…

I can't take it. "Go home, BOTH of you!" I scream.

An odd, but also familiar, pattern evolves in Roberto's behavior: Amorous entreaties alternating predictably with rages. The tantrums are followed by one of three possibilities. He displays aggrieved, but tearless, contrition. Or Roberto demands instant sex. Or he leaves for hours with uncertainty as to where he is going and when I'd see him again. Roberto is secretive and I never exactly know his whereabouts.

He is a romantic Don Juan who passionately loves and adores me, and then he suddenly rips me down and hates me. Sometimes it seems to happen so fast that both occur all at once.

"Her pull instantly shifts into a violent push and I am thrown to the floor."

He sees me as a reflection of himself: We are both racial mixes and renegades from the elite. He sees me as the odious other: an American capitalist, who must atone for my collective cultural sins.

Roberto is constantly suspicious and testing me. I've just run my daily two miles around the Olympic stadium and finished my two hours of calisthenics, wearing only underpants that pass as shorts. Another of Roberto's entourage of infinite friends, a beautiful young woman who I don't know, is chatting with him downstairs.

"Miguelito! Come downstairs and meet my friend, Lisa!" Roberto says in a loud voice. Half naked and still sweating, I stop midway down the stairs. Both Roberto and Lisa are staring at me from the bottom of the staircase and I feel embarrassed. I apologize for not having a shirt on…

"Oh, no! Don't get dressed, Miguelito. Lisa, what do you think of my cousin?"

"Oh, my God. He's absolutely gorgeous!" Roberto is not smiling and I feel his tension and envy. He's testing me again and I don't want another three-way.

Roberto is macho; he is argumentative, defensive, and always right. Sometimes his anger and stubbornness is helpful, like haggling for the price of groceries at the crowded open-air marketplace. Sometimes, his sense of entitlement scares me. We're in a store and I see something I'd like, but I don't have the money on me. Roberto slips the item into his pocket. "Everybody steals. Just chat with the cashier while I slip by and wait outside." It's OK—he's a Marxist. There should not be stores and private property, anyway.

I hate the ice-cold showers without a water heater, the toilet bowl without a seat, and the windows without screens. Roberto won't let me get hot water— "It makes a man stronger to take cold showers." Roberto won't let me get a toilet seat— "There's no need for a faggot toilet seat." Roberto won't help me tape wire mesh over the windows— "Just get used to the mosquitoes, you wimp!"

"House slaves were servants who had to adapt to their master's 'ways' and always gratify his will."

I feel confused by his rough machismo mixed with his tender amorousness. Under the distorted up and down reflections, the paranoid suspicions, the rages and tears, I cease to think logically. Roberto's tirades get worse. I am losing my freedom of speech and independent thought, engulfed by his non-negotiable worldview. I feel squeezed into becoming a facsimile of Roberto, or else damned as "against" him.

Now I need Roberto even more totally present to protect me because I'm so dependent on him. I feel like I can't do anything on my own and I need his permission to do anything at all. He is abusive, so I want him to go and leave me alone to fend for myself, and then I miss his protection and company. It's a seesaw and a yo-yo and a boomerang of the same old familiar pattern since my childhood—my mother.

Eventually, a financial reality creeps in: I am unable to get paid work, for political reasons. I am running out of money and I cannot support Roberto and myself any longer. My parents' letters reason that I must come home and at least finish my internship so I'd get a medical license in the States. My mother is worried about me, terribly worried.

Roberto does finally cry, and so does Silvia, when my departure plane arrives. I lie and say I'm coming back real soon. But I feel fearful and ambivalent here. Colombia is collapsing and it breaks my heart.

Roberto will come, just once, and visit me in California for a couple of weeks.

Gringo-Landia is not like the Disney-Landia stereotype; it's more complex than Rob had realized. There are an awful lot of non-blond people from all around the world here. And a lot of poor people, too. He'll still be paranoid, jealous, and angry, a *cimarrón* and Casanova who I'll have a three-way with once more.

I will return two years later to see Roberto in Colombia for a few weeks. He will lambast me in front of some cousins about having abandoned him, having lied saying I'd come back to stay, and for being a mercenary capitalist. As before, I will be reduced to tears. But that will be the last time I'll see Roberto.

Silvia will have lost her ranch, accosted and forcibly evicted by a band of thugs who claimed indigenous rights to the confiscated property. There will be no court to appeal to. Roberto's mother will never get the government pension she is owed from her husband's death. There will be no judge to award it. The drug mafia will overrun Cali and its port, Buenaventura; friends and acquaintances I knew there will be murdered. There will be no jury to convict the murderers.

Roberto will show me the ruins of the Supreme Court building where his father once served. Rebels captured and executed the justices, and then dynamited the building into rubble a year ago. There will be no effort to rebuild the Hall of Justice. Helicopters swarm overhead and brigades of army men will march and trot in formation down the streets. You cannot travel beyond a fifty-kilometer radius from any major city in Colombia. The nation is under perpetual siege.

There's not much left of the once proud Latin Capitol of Culture and Democracy. The new "Colombian capitalists" rule without reins or regrets. They are the drug lords of the world. Roberto won't send any more odes of love to me. He will call me and beg for money instead. I will not be able to give him money the last time he calls. Then, I will be a "fucking selfish American capitalist".

Maybe Roberto's distrust is cultural, or Afro-cultural, or a part of his Latin machismo. Maybe that's understandable, given his upbringing and circumstances. Maybe Roberto is truly paranoid.

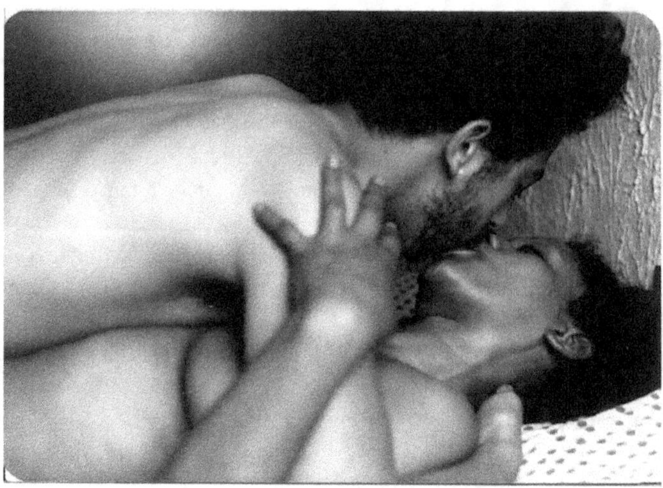

A threesome:
Roberto and Silvia are in the photograph.
I am the photographer.

This compelling story about my third—and longest—marriage relates to the basis of corruption in the business ethos with both sociopathic and narcissistic elements.

In a heterogeneous mixture of "greatness" and "unworthiness," I would try, but always fail, to improve my self-esteem. The two qualities were a set-up for failure, as the very word "try" connotes. I carried the stature of innate intelligence, an impressive academic record and a lofty professional degree, so I could *look proud*. I would hammer my body into the shape of an Adonis to fortify my attractive physical appearance, so I could *look good*. But nothing gave me any lasting, positive self-image.

Instead, the attributes of achievement and looking proud and looking good attracted social predators and narcissists. Sometimes, I started the tragic relationship by approaching a self-assured narcissist to help me feel more secure, or mistaking him or her for my equal. Soon, I was hopelessly entangled in his web. Narcissists all exude a bloated confidence that is easy to fall for. I'd attach myself to the great man or woman, operating behind the scenes, like Rasputin and Czar Nicolas II. I would be their hidden confidant and genius.

I would then loyally sacrifice myself for my partner, with the empty promise of material riches or social status. I would support my dominant partner like a house slave or a very oppressed housewife of the 1950's. I would alter my life's mission to create their greatness and fulfill their quest for power and glory, existing only as their "eco." For a while, I would enjoy vicarious power, leadership, success, and belongingness, but only as a mere escort and appendage of my partner's ego.

All such relationships led to devastating exploitation, stripping me of the promised security and status to a point much lower than what I'd originally had. When I was of no further use to them, when they had strip-mined all the ore of my resources and exploited the fertile land of my gifts, narcissists would discard me without compunction.

"When the slaves could not work anymore, they were thrown into these crocodile pits for amusement."

Or, if I pulled myself back to sanity, back to my true self, and they could no longer "possess" me, they had to destroy me as a rival. I have learned that most of those who appear to be great may just be only that: an appearance. Narcissists abound, and show-offs who deny they have any vulnerability are narcissists until proven otherwise.

"Mirror, mirror, on the wall" …

My "Narcissist Collection" of intimate relationships is epitomized in the following memoir. It depicts my longest relationship, one that I grieved for many years as I peeled away the abuse, layer by layer, like a Napoleon pastry— a *gâteau de mille-feuilles*, a cake of a thousand leaves...

*

BEST IN SHOW
My 3rd marriage…

I'm twenty-seven. I've just finished my medical internship in Oakland and I have two months to look for a job and find a partner. I've dated and had many sex-mates, but nobody feels just right. Maybe the *bar scene* is the wrong venue?

I'm attending a gay men's *discussion group* at the Pacific Center in Berkeley. At least here, I can have a moment—a sound bite—to speak and maybe somebody will like me for my intelligence and not just my looks. Thomas is one of the twenty participants in the group tonight. As soon as the discussion is open, he speaks up first.

He's English, and I am attracted to foreigners because they usually don't carry the racial baggage of Americans. Thomas is tall, but plain looking; he has a sharp mind and seems intense. At the end of the group, I go over to meet him. "Hi. I liked what you said…." I initiate the conversation sheepishly.

"Oh, OK. I was *more* interested in the Mormon fellow over there, but you were second on my list of people to talk to. He's busy with other guys, anyway."

Thomas begins to enthrall me with his social conscience. He plans to donate ten percent of his business profits to "black causes" like literacy programs to teach black mothers in the South to read to their children, money to fight apartheid in South Africa, and scholarships for gifted black students.

Over the next eleven years, Thomas and I will grow up together, but not grow together. He has had a painful life and he wants a rich life to compensate.

Thomas was born to an evil, paranoid mother who beat him with the rod of the vacuum cleaner. He, in turn, emotionally abused his only sibling, a younger sister. They were very poor; his father had lied about his true age and only lived for ten years after marrying—just enough time to produce the two fatherless children. When his father died, Thomas' mother lost her job as head nurse at a Methodist teaching hospital because unwed women were not acceptable for employment there. She went on the dole; that means she had to live on welfare in Britain.

I can't remember the mother's first name. Was it "Ruth" perhaps? She was just, "My Mum." In fact, scarcely *anybody* knew her first name. Once she was given an apron with her initials sewn on it; she unstitched them so her neighbors could never even *guess* what her first name was. She wouldn't allow any familiarity with strangers.

We arrive in England to visit his mother and pick up Thomas' costly Green Card. Thomas has not seen his mother for five years. At the agreed-upon time, we are at her small house that faces the open hills of Westminster. But she is not at home.

Thomas is excited to revisit his past. "Look! Through this window is where my bedroom was. And here's the kitchen." He adds quietly, "Oh, my, nothing's changed."

An hour later, we are still locked outside and sitting in the small back garden. The figure of a woman looms on the treeless green grass ridge. "Is that Mum?" Thomas can't be sure. Slowly the woman gets within recognizable range. She has a dog on a leash and walks stiffly using a cane.

"It's Mum! And that's my dog! HELLO, MUM!" he shouts ecstatically out to the hilltop in the distance.

The woman hollers back, lifting both her walking stick and the leashed dog menacing high into the air, "STOP IT! **STOP IT!** You're exciting the dog!"

Thomas mutters, again, "Oh, my, nothing's changed."

We remain in grim silence until Mum arrives at the cottage and glares at her son, then at me. "Well, I suppose you'll be wanting some tea," she grumbles. She turns away and enters the cottage as a stern, stiff hulk that sends shivers down my spine. Later, Thomas will try to engage her, as will I. He will have no success; I will have *some*—until years later when Thomas will tell her that he's gay and we're a couple.

Thomas talks about a book describing near-death and afterlife experiences, and gives his mother a copy. She sits with it for five minutes in a private study. Then she storms back into the living room and hurls the book full velocity at her son in rage. "POPPYCOCK!"

She has severe tremors in her hands and is having her eighth cup of tea for the evening. Thomas suggests that maybe the caffeine is too much for her. "NONSENSE! There's no caffeine in tea. It's *English* tea!" Mum shouts.

Abrupt end of subject and soon the end of indescribable misery with my vow to never, *ever*, encounter the old witch again. I feel more sympathy for Thomas now; it's not his fault, he's not to blame. He's just so unlucky.

Unpredictable or unreliable care-giving from one's parents and severe emotional abuse in childhood…

I just didn't realize that it could cause a predisposed genetic condition.

Thomas is determined to get rich, *fabulously* rich. He's dreamt of unlimited wealth his whole life. He never attended college or acquired professional skills; therefore, he became a businessman. He was a "townie" who grew up near the elitist Harrow Academy; Harrow is to Eaton like Exeter is to Andover. Townsfolk called it: "Harrow on the

Hill." Thomas grew up "beneath the hill" and could only watch the fortunate students above him.

Thomas has a terrible envy of the English ruling class. He's even thought of changing his first name to "Sir" so that, in America, people would call him that and he'd get away with being a lord or a knight. The title of "Baron" is currently on the market for sale; it would cost about one million dollars and Thomas is seriously considering buying one.

Thomas left home and started working at age seventeen. He crammed the *Wall Street Journal,* the *Manchester Guardian Weekly,* and *Le Monde*—filling his mind with all the data that he believed would ensure his wealth. Thomas still reads constantly, carrying magazines and articles wherever we go. He truly thinks that he can arm himself with enough information to impress *anybody,* to master the world and get the wealth he craves.

He is convinced—and very *convincing*—that his start-up company will soon rise to dominate the field of "empathy products." He compares his company to Pepsi-Cola competing with Coca-Cola. But he tends to push just a little bit too fast to get there.

He first got into trouble for "borrowing" merchandise from an office supply store in England where he was a young manager. He fled from England to Africa to escape jail for theft, and started the fugitive travelogue of his life. There were great fables and stories of crossing the Sahara by land, fat women falling into crocodile-filled lakes off an over-loaded ferry in Rhodesia, or waiting days for buses to fill up before leaving and trains that were never on time. Soon he got into trouble with the law again. He fled Rhodesia to avoid jail for smuggling. "But everybody else was doing it. I just got caught," he rationalizes.

Thomas would only tell me about these felony convictions in the sixth year of our marriage, to explain why he had to spend such a fortune to get a Green Card, under false self-representation and using an elaborate scheme.

After fleeing Rhodesia, he arrived in South Africa where he could live in a style that suited him. He could drop his clothes randomly through the house to force his black servants to pick up after him. Finally, he came to America, the land of opportunity on a Green Card that soon expired. He believed that his English accent would impress Americans who would not be able to tell that it was a working-class accent, unlike in England where his accent betrayed his humbler origin.

Thomas has fantasies of owning private palaces, private jets, private train cars, and private everything. Yet Thomas does not respect other's private property. A "No Trespassing" sign compels him to jump the fence, saying that in England there are established rights-of-way and Americans have *no* right to block his path. I sometimes follow him as ordered, but very nervously—like under the turn-style gate of the Metro in Paris years before.

In fact, I shake with fear when Thomas breaches the law. He doesn't seem to understand that what a *white* man can get away with, a *black* man can't. Yet I follow him over the fences and barriers because I am linked to his will and dependent on his proximity.

Thomas takes up a franchise of an English-based accelerated reading group, like Evelyn Woods, and then locates a schoolteacher in the Midwest who has an innovative reading program and has invented a new reading methodology. He calls her and, with his English accent and a false pretense, he soon charms her into sending him the whole program for free. "To help the poor students," he says to her, impersonating being a schoolteacher.

That night he celebrates and skips, singing through the house. He rejoices at his good fortune and jokes about the stupidity of the teacher to not have had it all protected by a copyright. That was the happiest I ever saw my beloved. Armed with new material, he breaks his agreement with the English-run franchise like the Bostonians repudiated the English at the Boston Tea Party.

Then he commences his business-based strategy: Find smart, creative people, get them to invent and deliver programs, and collect the profits. He seduces the best teachers to work for him and to produce courses for his company. The money pours in, but then he must have *more*.

He spends a million dollars on a far-shot gamble, a scheme from an eccentric genius consultant—a ruse to break through to the CEOs of major corporations. It involves creating the "perfect letter" that could lift Excalibur's Sword of resistance by hypnotizing, wooing, and manipulating the personal assistant of the CEO. "She's the gate-keeper. If I can win *her* over, the CEO will fall into my hands!"

Thomas has a way of getting First Class treatment without having to pay for it. He makes me wait before boarding a flight until the last second before the ramp doors close. Then, he rushes in with me panting behind him, to grab empty first class seats…. "They never ask!"

We are on a steep trail at Mount Helena and Thomas sees the signs: "Dogs on Leash Only." He's inherited the dog I'd raised, before he kicked me out of our house. The dog is now an extension of Thomas and therefore it is above the law. The dog is skipping loose on the mountain fire road when a ranger's jeep turns around a bend in front of us, and the ranger spots the unleashed dog.

'It's just a small fine and Thomas will just have to pay it,' I think. In a flash, Thomas has kicked the innocent dog off the cliff and thrown himself over the ledge *en suite*, sliding down out of sight. I remain standing on the road in shock, hoping neither my ex-puppy nor my now ex-partner have broken a leg. The ranger slams the brakes to a dead stop, and Thomas climbs back up carrying the dog, *caught red-handed.*

"I've never seen anything like this," the Ranger exclaims.

I proceed to apologize for my friend's behavior, and Thomas starts to kick my shins violently. "LET *ME* DO THE TALKING!" When he gets the $15 ticket, Thomas is so enraged with me for betraying him that he sulks and refuses to speak a word to me during the hour's climb back down to our cars and away.

Thomas must be the boss and rule his world with unquestioned authority. He must be admired as the center and the top of the world, because he is *always* right. Thomas also believes that he deserves only the best, and he obsesses and argues about "what's the best" and incessantly categorizes the "best of the best" of everything.

His dogs are the best; in fact, they are reincarnations of great Buddhist monks who came back by divine choice to be with him. He takes them to the best dog psychic to communicate with them, because he doesn't have any friends. He finds the world's best psychotherapist and claims that after a short course of sessions he was told he was the best client the therapist has ever had, and he is completely cured of all past traumas and issues.

He demands the best dining, the best suits, and the best connections. There are the best theater shows and seats, and the best places to travel. He must have the best automobile, the best non-toxic carpeting, and the best stolen Buddha—smuggled out of Cambodia in defiance of international trade agreements.

The "best deals..."

"He can argue the leg off a lamb!" his mother told me in England.

After years of scorning the stupid idea of meditation, he decides to excel at meditation and become enlightened. He manages to get a seat on the board of directors of a Buddhist retreat center, which permits the "royal we." "At Spirit Rock, *we* don't approve of…." In his mind, the center now belongs to him, and since he is on the board, he is assuredly an enlightened being.

"Show Time" is the way Thomas gets to be popular with his employees and be the center of admiration. There are costume parties, gala events with jazz bands and comedians, and antique Bentleys and Rolls Royce's that pop up out-of-the-blue to limousine his staff to the best restaurants. Thomas rents the Goodyear blimp for a day's excursion, soaring over the Golden Gate Bridge, up the coast, over whales, and around the Bank of America pyramid—with champagne and *hors d'oevres* and toasts exalting him and his company. Or he rents a huge three-mast sailing ship to watch the Fourth of July fireworks from the bay…or a private train coach like in "The Wild, Wild West" TV series for an impressive party riding up into the Sierras.

"Home Time" is when Thomas withholds love. Thomas is only fleetingly happy when he gets his way or gets stoned or gets a new business scheme that rekindles his fantasy of unlimited wealth. Sometimes, he does show love. That's when he's under the influence of the love drug—Ecstasy. But it's a chemical love, which is forced immediately back into the vortex of another dimension when the chemical wears off. Sometimes, with loud music and marijuana, he skips a bit and cracks Monty Python lines. I thought I loved Thomas during such moments, but that effect didn't last, either.

He finds a bargain "genius" gardener to finish the backyard. I am thrilled with the project, following every detail with glee. His "best" garden is featured in "Sunset Magazine" and "Home and Garden" and wins several awards. Thomas takes credit for it because he paid for the gardener.

Eventually, Thomas decides that his greatest skill is to judge all people and all things. He then embarks on a costly failure. As usual, he hires his chosen experts to tap their brains. This time, they will rank every small business and annual event in the county, and then Thomas will have a book ghostwritten on the "Best of the Best of the County." The book will not earn him the money and fame he expects, but odium and spite from most of the merchants in his community. In response, he becomes more cantankerous, bitter, and isolated. He becomes more like his "Mum."

We trek to Alaska, Hawaii, Vermont, and the San Juan Islands off Seattle. There are camping trips to the Southwest and up into the Sierras. Every month includes a hot springs resort for a long weekend at the best hot springs. Thomas likes to explore but he isn't an easy travel companion. Everywhere we go, Thomas is condescending to staff; he is demanding, impatient, and complaining. He *hates* inferior quality and poor, dirty places. The interior of Mexico and the Arctic appall him.

Thomas is non-sexual and not physically romantic. He never cuddles or lets me touch him in bed. The loneliness becomes unbearable. Year after year, my isolation grows and drives me to seek outside friendships and sex partners, all of whom Thomas dismisses as far beneath him.

We travel to Yellowstone National Park and arrive at our cabin late one summer night. In the morning, for the first time, I think that Thomas is sending me a long-awaited bio-message that he is sexually turned on to me. As almost always, I initiate. The musky, lusty hormones are so powerful that the cabin seems to vibrate with hedonistic rhythm. After sex, I open the drapes and see that a herd of bison has surrounded the cabin and they are rubbing against the cabin's walls to scratch their sides. It was only the bison's energy I'd been sensing; Thomas hasn't changed at all.

Thomas listens to me talk for a while over dinner, but he's looking at his watch. Then he explodes. "That's enough! I've been listening to *you* for half an hour!" he yells. "Don't you think you should ask me about *my* day?" But Thomas has been telling me about his day all day long, and I've been listening intently because he is a great and noble man who will make a fortune and take care of me for the rest of my life.

Every day I try to please Thomas. I shower him with surprises and gifts. Fresh flowers always adorn the hallways and dining room table. I buy and finish furniture and design exquisite draperies to decorate the living room. I frame his paintings by hand; I pour cement floors in the basement, and I create unforgettable Christmases with so many gifts lavished on him that it takes two days to open them all.

I supervise the regular house staff: private cooks, daily maids, and gardeners, who Thomas scorns and whose tears I console. The household burden falls on my shoulders, unappreciated and unrewarded; Thomas is too important for such tedious things.

Most of the time, Thomas is stoned and blockaded behind a newspaper spread in front of his face, with the angry admonishment, "Don't interrupt me! I'm reading!" He ignores me as he spends more and more time reading or daydreaming. Thomas scoffs at my interest in exercise, languages, spirituality, and especially my medical practice. Nothing matters outside of his world, *unless* lots of money is involved.

Eventually Thomas' rages become hostile and then hateful, and his tirades against me are constant. Every social engagement leads to Thomas's scolding me about my imperfect performance. I now work for his company, for which he pays me half of what he pays other trainers, and scolds me if even one of the student evaluations is less the "The best trainer I've ever had." - Thomas demands A+ reviews—nothing ever less, or else I am ruining *his* glorious future. He makes scenes in public, chastising me for training the dog, "*My* dog doesn't need training!"

"MY daughter doesn't need public school!"

He drives his BMW, the best sports model, speeding furiously through the city and country, always eager to honk the horn and make pedestrians scramble. He pours me the best wine to drink in crystal wine glasses with him while he drives the car. "It's not against the law in *England!"*

I am always on edge. I split with a sort of psychotic uncertainty until I literally cannot do or say anything, not utter a word nor move a foot, until told to do so. I vacillate: If I say that, he will trounce me; if I don't say that, he will trounce me. I become tongue tied and choked as he condemns every statement and behavior as "stupid" or "wrong." I question the validity or utility of all my experience, knowledge, and intuitions.

I become an appendage to his ego at home and an attractive escort in public. I learn to keep quiet. I learn to stay out of his way, and stay drunk, while he stays stoned. I am reaching the "freeze" point of toxic shame with Thomas. I live in the sheer hell of being gagged by and double bound to a pure narcissist.

After years of spending sprees and almost unlimited wealth, Thomas' luck turns sour. His courses are way overpriced. His reputation is not good and his competition gives successful lower bids to corporate customers—even though "they deliver inferior products and training." Many of his employees leave disgruntled. Using property zoned for residential purposes for his business is reported. The economy changes and the training and consulting field can't command exorbitant fees for two-day seminars anymore. Interactive computer training takes over; it's much more cost-effective. Thomas becomes desperate. As his wealth dissipates, he becomes increasingly cold and aloof and I become increasingly lonely.

Finally, the turning point comes. Perhaps I crossed the line when I bring home another Englishman on New Year's Eve. Thomas has told me to "go find sex elsewhere" because he doesn't have a sex drive. But *this* time, Thomas goes crazy and decides to exact revenge. I don't remember much of the last six months of abject surrender to punishment; I stayed drunk most of the time.

My new English boyfriend finds out that he had AIDS. I stop seeing him and sink, deeper and deeper, into depression. The more depressed I feel…the happier Thomas appears to be. His schemes turn onto me. He must have money, *all* the money to maintain his lifestyle. Besides, *everything* is, theoretically or in his mind, all his anyway. My ten years of service and all my material goods belong exclusively to him, and furthermore Thomas justifies that he *needs* money more than me.

He discovers a ruse to get our duplex converted into two separate saleable units, which will vastly increase the property value. I work hard to oversee the inspectors, making sure all goes well. Then, Thomas tells me that having two names on the deed is blocking the city's approval; he convinces me that I must relinquish my part of the title for it to go through the system.

I trust Thomas and the million-dollar house—and all its expensive contents—become entirely his in early August 1992. In late August, I am working out of town doing a rural medical assignment for a couple of weeks. The house in San Francisco is on the market, and Thomas and I have been looking at new property to buy in the countryside. I hope that a new home, away from the place of so much sorrow and trauma, will "cure" us both. We find a house I like very much, but Thomas balks and insists on something *better.*

He is biding time, until just the right—the "perfect"—moment.

"Better" could mean many things in his schemes.

I still deeply love and I trust my partner…

I clean up my act, stop drinking, swear off external affairs, and I'm making good money to contribute to the household. The day I leave the rural hotel room to return home, my parents call me and say they have a grand surprise for me, and under no circumstances should I go back home to Thomas before seeing them first.

The surprise is that Thomas has thrown me out and told my parents to come and pick up the few things that he will allow me to have or he didn't want. My parents have rented a small basement apartment on the fringe of a regional ghetto, into which they have crammed my private belongings and my mismatched pieces of leftover furniture, following my mother's floor plan, of course. My parents have happily reclaimed my prodigal soul. They tell me that I should be grateful for the surprise, and for Thomas' and their own hard work.

Thomas always believed that I was almost "the best," so he kept me around until he decided it was in his "better" interest to get rid of me. He said that he planned to find somebody considerably better than me by screening out a couple of flaws and adjusting a few variables in a careful international headhunt search. But that would never happen—Thomas could not find a better replacement. People are more challenging to rate than pet grooming salons and dentists and bookstores. He would be doomed to living single and eschew almost all dating for the rest of his life—*nobody* was good enough. He would likely replicate his aloof mother, alone and friendless until the end.

He's lost a lot. His sister committed suicide due to her horrible childhood of abuse by both her mother and Thomas—abuse that had left her unable to have the joy of any intimate relationship. His mother finally died, leaving a pittance to her son. His perfect purebred dog died young. The perfect mixed breed replacement dog from the pound died young.

Thomas sees himself as a brilliant victim, a gifted expert in the art of listening and empathy, endowed with a generous and philanthropic heart. He has memorized the lines and phrases to say to *affect* empathy, but he only listens for content that he can exploit or accrue to his ego. He cannot see himself as a narcissist, for that implies an imperfection. To even mention that he might be narcissistic incites *narcissistic rage* and a counter-accusation of the speaker of being narcissistic instead.

It would take me ten years to recover from the relationship after the end of our domestic partnership in 1992. My self-doubt overcame my self-esteem. During the ensuing decade, I would decide that it was in *my* best interest to not look for high-achievers anymore. I would look for "lessers," hoping that they might not reject me and they could reciprocate my love.

I saw Thomas for the last time about one year ago. He was effusive and demanded physical hugs, but I held back. He bragged that the lamb dinner he'd cooked was perfect, but it was not. He wanted me to drink wine and get stoned, and I declined. He was living completely alone in his private, splendid countryside estate, struggling with his losses, yet simultaneously boasting. "Well, I'm glad Obama is the president. So far, he's doing everything right. He's doing everything that *I* would do as president!"

Then he became disgruntled—I was not falling into his fan club like usual. I refused to give him his "narcissistic supply." I did not flatter his ego or automatically comply with his expectations. Although I didn't put him down, the *absence* of flattery and admiration was a terrible offense; this time, I suspect Thomas will never speak to me again. Later, I realized that Thomas had never said the words, "I'm sorry." I guess that's because he was perfect and never wrong.

This odd relationship seems to stand out of context with all my other marriages, although I remain a codependent caretaker, but settling for less and desperate for love—from the most unsuitable partner possible.

EXTRAORDINARILY ORDINARY
My 4ᵗʰ marriage…

After three foiled relationships, I decide to reverse my relationship-hunting logic. My previous, ten-year relationship as Eco in the alcoves of Narcissism is over, my self-esteem has been smashed, and I feel I cannot survive alone.

I go to a bar in the Castro on a rainy fall night. It's a gay bar that caters to older guys, sometimes referred to pejoratively as "The Open Casket." It's too crowded to sit, except for one seat where two elderly men are chatting. With them is an odd-looking fellow; he's a short, gnome-like, and very quiet man, about my age of thirty-seven years, with long brown hair down to his mid-back.

Russ is clearly *not* my type. Therefore, I conclude that he might be good for me. My type has led to narcissistic predators, so I reason that I should look for *non*-appealing partners instead. He seems simple-minded and ingenuous. He speaks very little, so I must initiate and maintain the conversation with questions.

Russ moved to the redwood forests of Guerneville, the gay Mecca on the Russian River, about a year ago. He lives in a trailer park in the woods, alone, not reading, not doing much…just thinking a lot. He got a job managing a gas station where he generally sits in the office and sometimes pumps gas.

He's had no formal education, but he is sure he could learn anything, if he tries. He doesn't miss his family back East. They were OK with his leaving. He's had very little relationship experience—in fact, none, really.

Maybe he has a friend. He points to one of the older guys who'd accompanied him. The fellow lives in the adjacent trailer. They'd sometimes sit and watch TV together. Russ likes TV; it's new to him. There was a fellow he'd had oral sex with, but no strong feelings. He'd had sex with a girl or two and it was OK. But she got attached and he didn't like that. Probably he prefers men, or maybe it doesn't matter much.

He was too scared to drive from the woods into the big city of San Francisco today, so he got his older neighbor to drive for him—*just a friend*, he repeats. Cars go too fast. He's just spilled his first drink on his trousers, and, no, he hasn't peed on himself. Then he laughs, or more accurately, he giggles a moment before his plain face goes blank again.

He's had to escape the restrictions of his socially backward, small village community out East when he discovered that he was probably gay. He likes to ride horses and is a great jockey. He can ride bareback and barefoot. He knows about farming. He doesn't have any hobbies.

And, he's *Amish*. "I've never met a black man before," he comments. I wrangle him away from his friends; we go out for a hamburger and then to my apartment for the night.

I've already made some grand plans after the ending of my long previous relationship. I have been accepted into the Master's in public health program at Johns Hopkins University in Baltimore, together with a prestigious fellowship in Nigeria after the MPH year. The program begins in the spring, so I have six months with no obligations and some savings. Why not take my savings and live in Costa Rica for a few months?

The only thing missing is somebody with whom to share my new life. I mention my plans to Russ and get no reaction. I want a travel companion and a partner, but Russ seems more the former. I have a few concerns, one being his strange affect and the other that he has never had any foreign travel experience. He reminds me that he's Amish and they don't approve of such things. It takes two months of visiting me before I can convince him to apply for a passport. I must coach him every step of the way; it seems like he came straight out of the 1800s, a modern Rip Van Winkle character.

Soon I chaperone my new companion into realms that he could neither imagine nor accommodate in his mind. I *feel* that I am in love with him, and I find reasons to appreciate him and give him encouragement and compliments.

Russ calms down from the terror of his first air travel when we get off the plane in San Juan, Costa Rica. Even though he was petrified during the flight, his answers to questions were only the bare nuts-and-bolts of neutrality.

"How are you *feeling*, Russ?"
"I'm fine."

"What are you *thinking*, Russ?"
"Nothing. Just looking."

We arrive at the ultimate destination: Volcano Arenal in northwestern Costa Rica. I rent a ten-acre ranch with a quaint three-bedroom house from whose windows I see a pristine blue lake below and the volcano a couple of miles away, towering over the lake. It's awe-inspiring! Hourly booms, like Old Faithful Geyser, furiously rattle the house's windows, in tandem with jettisoning a spellbinding, blasting plume of smoke and fire from its summit.

"It's nice," Russ comments.

The ranch-hands saddle up the two horses and we ride everywhere—into town, around the lake, into the forest filled with Howler monkeys, and over hillsides bursting with wild orchids. Wherever one gazes, there is magnificent fauna and flora, in endless successions of indescribable beauty.

"It's OK," mumbles Russ.

I befriend a Belgian shepherd at a lakeside resort. The dog runs devotedly behind the transit bus *en route* back to our rented house. The four-legged animal trails farther and farther behind the bus, exhausted, and then he disappears as the bus speeds away for the next five miles. Half an hour later, I see the dog panting as he climbs up the hill to the front porch of my house, and then he jumps onto my lap. From then on, he shows up every morning to escort Russ and me on our horseback excursions or just to hang out with me. 'The dog has more emotion than Russ,' I think.

Russ is sexually inexperienced, so I teach him what I can. It's the only time I feel his presence and I try to believe that it's "love." I praise Russ, and then I start to criticize Russ. I try to solicit Russ' opinions, feelings, wants, and I fail.

We're riding through a vast meadow near the cliffs at the lake's shoreline. It's a familiar path with tall grass and wildflowers. As usual, Russ is on the fast and wild horse because he's OK with such. I'm on the middle-aged, pot-bellied mare, because she's as easy on me as I am on her. Suddenly Russ' mount rears up and gallops like mad to the cliff's edge, then leaps off the twenty-foot embankment, literally flying in the air, before plummeting into the lake!

I hurry over to the top of the cliff to see if Russ is safe. He answers placidly from below, "The horse saw a snake."

Slowly, Russ becomes *more* than quiet; his face is getting angry although he denies having anger. His movements are becoming brusque, especially when I am happy and chatting in Spanish to the locals, making friends and making plans. The locals ask me, "What's wrong with your companion?" They notice the obvious grimace of tight-lipped hostility, as do I, and it frightens them.

After Costa Rica, we drive across the USA, from San Francisco to Baltimore. On the way, to kill idle hours, I chatter about the Theory of Relativity and mysticism and...

"I know all about it! Don't talk so much!" Russ snaps back. In a motel, mid-way, I break down, telling Russ that he's not right, not treating me right, and *"Please show me some love!"* He asks me to fuck him. That is the only time Russ initiated sex or any form of tactile intimacy whatsoever.

It's the first night in our third-floor apartment in the impoverished inner city of Baltimore. There are blocks after blocks of rundown brick apartment buildings that were once, like in the heart of so many decaying inner cities, a marvel of elegance and beauty. Suddenly I hear sounds outside my window that alarm me...

"NO! Don't do it! They'll *catch* you!" a woman's voice begs.

I bolt up in bed, listening to the sounds of running footsteps, then a terrible breaking of glass, and then an explosion like the volcano but *too close*. The apartment building kiddy-corner from us has burst into flames—firebombed! Lives are at stake. Terrified residents are pouring out with children and pets. I try to wake Russ up, but he turns away in bed and jams his earplugs in harder. I pull them out and shout, *"The building over there is BURNING! I heard…"*

Russ is angry and pushes me away.

"Leave me alone! I'm sleeping," he grumbles.

Russ will get a job as a house painter. He will also get more and more taciturn, sullen, and hateful. He will refuse to talk to me or support my studies in Baltimore. The domestic union will be reduced to a mere household.

And he will *hate* Baltimore, and he will *hate* me for taking him to a foreign land and a big city. Soon I will give him my car so he can drive back to Guerneville, where he will live alone once again in a trailer in a forest and work at a gas station.

I will see him one last time when I drive up to the gas station on the Russian River. "What do *you* want? Why are *you* here?" he glares at me with cold hate.

"I'm sorry, I just wanted to see you. I'm *sorry* about Baltimore."

"It's all *forgotten*," he replies.

I quickly drive away.

*

Perhaps I can meet a good partner by going back to school?

The following excerpt depicts my fifth marriage— the only one out of ten that was to a woman. The title: "Fashionable" is, of course, a double-entendre: the woman was indeed a "fashion designer" and she was also convinced that she could "fashion" me to her liking. The complexity of the subthemes is captured in the following synopsis: A nymphomaniac— who is determined to convert me from gay to straight— ensnares me into a marriage while I am in an altered, drugged state of consciousness.

She is a Sephardic Jewish English princess fashion designer with an eating disorder, working on her doctorate in clinical psychology. The character represents a Histrionic Personality Disorder, and an amorous narcissist—the female Don Juan or Casanova. The story is deep and funny, a tragic-comedy with poetic license. Details of my formal Jewish wedding are followed

by dramatic narrative about my honeymoon that takes place in Tahiti.

FASHIONABLE
My 5ᵗʰ marriage…

Jessica is forty-three and I am thirty-seven when we meet. It's the first day of a class on world religions at the California Institute for Integral Studies in San Francisco. I've decided to fill the void of my collapsing decade-long relationship with Art by studying religion. This is an alternative college with a good reputation, which caters mostly to new age and middle-aged renegades.

The fifteen-odd students are sitting in a semi-circle facing the instructor and the blackboard. I arrive late and take the last seat near the door. The woman in the end seat directly across from me seems to pay intense attention to my presence, as if transfixed by whatever I say in class. She has a pretty round face and wears ostentatious jewelry, make-up, and revealing clothing. Most female students here won't wear jewelry or make-up; such beautification is considered too mainstream. She has an odd accent; it's continental English, with a peculiar slurred twist of theatrical intonation and vagueness.

After class, she jumps up to introduce herself and chat with me on the way to my car. Within a minute I know a lot about her. Her name is Jessica and she's from the Yorkshire district of England. She's Sephardic Jewish on her mother's side, Ashkenazi Jewish on her father's. She's finishing her dissertation for a doctorate in clinical psychology. And she's single.

I tell her I'm gay and in a relationship. She invites me to her apartment for dinner the next week. Reluctantly, I accept the invitation, although I must check with Art and see if I'm obligated elsewhere. 'Is she coming on to me?' I wonder. Flattering, but foolish—yet, I'm curious about her.

After the second class, Jessica again escorts me out into the busy open courtyard of the school. I tell her something's come up and I can't go to her apartment for dinner this week, maybe the following week? Immediately her round face contorts into utter despair as she falls to her knees, bawling and looking up at me imploringly. "Don't *do* this to me! Oh, please, not *again!*" she wails.

I look down, speechless, at her plump pumpkin-round body that matches her cherry-round face. Tears gush onto her lovely dress and onto the pavement. Her make-up is streaking. People are watching us as if I'm abusing this poor woman who I hardly know. "OK! No problem, Jessica. *Please* stand up!" I bend over to help lift her up.

Over dinner, Jessica tells me more about her life story. She comes from a moderately wealthy family and has an older brother who is an Oxford-educated solicitor. He is financially *very* fortunate and has conformed to her parents' wishes. She, on the other hand, is rebellious toward her conservative parents and escaped England every summer, going alone to Greece when she was barely an adolescent.

One summer she put an ad in the paper to find three other women to accompany her on a first-ever world feat: They would bicycle across Europe, Yugoslavia, Turkey, Iran, over the Himalayas, and end in India. Two of her companions gave up, and the third died in the Himalayas.

In India, she learned to wear flowing robes—or nothing at all in the nudist colony where she landed. Between the two dressing styles, she invented an exotic clothing design and opened a shop in the most elegant fashion district of London. She shows me a copy of "Vogue" with her pretty plump face on the cover to make sure I believe her.

She continues her story. Her Sephardic gypsy ancestors fled from the Spanish Inquisition because they risked being burnt at the stake as witches. They populated the Ottoman Empire in Turkey, where she has relatives who might *still* be witches. Jessica believes in witchcraft and psychics; her best friend, one of too many who rarely calls or even remembers her, is a "renowned psychic." Jessica tells me that he can read the future perfectly. As proof, he has $50,000 or more stuffed under his bed, just from his last business trip alone! He sees clients who wait for him worldwide.

But Jessica has issues. She has a body-image issue: She is squat and stocky like her Sephardic ancestors. She has a male-bonding issue: Her smarter, older brother and his buddy group had taunted and scorned her as a stupid little girl. She has a money issue: Her father died tragically and her mother's last wish is to see her only daughter properly married and financially well-off.

She winks at me as she adds, "And I'm into black men." Jessica is mesmerizing, tantalizing, and seductive. She knows I'm gay and partnered. I feel awkward; she's turning me on and this is not what I'm used to. I'm not very attracted to her, but she wants me so badly...

I finish off the second bottle of wine and follow Jessica to her bedroom to "see her wardrobe." The next thing I know is that I'm making love to her and it feels good.

And so, it is for the next six months; intermittent soirees with my mistress, whose emotional changes are abrupt, yet shallow. Jessica would cry, then laugh, then rage, and I feel increasingly enmeshed with her like I'd felt with my mother. 'Is allowing her seductions like *trying to please my mother*, too?' I ask myself.

I introduce Jessica to my partner. They are both English, so they should get along. Art notices her accent immediately; it conveys her bourgeois status as belonging to the upper middle-class, or possibly the lower upper class, as well as Jewish and Yorkshire. Then, he whispers to me, "That's the sort of woman I'd *never* dare cross."

Jessica marvels at my house, especially the house staff. "So, you have a cook and a maid, *every day?*" She just loves the atmosphere of wealth.

"I'm still uncomfortable having all this help here," I reply.

"Well, you'll just have to get used to it!" she advises.

Jessica takes me to her synagogue. Afterwards, the valet-parked cars are brought one by one up to the temple's front steps, which are crowded with waiting owners. When my car, or truthfully, my partner's "best" BMW rolls up, Jessica chortles and waltzes with an arrogant stride to the vehicle and waits for me to open her door.

"How do you think I fit in as a 'black Jew' at the synagogue?" I ask her.

"I don't know, but they *really* liked your car!"

Then, Jessica would act drunk on one glass of wine at my house and say she can't drive home. I set her up in the guest bedroom and tuck her in. She tearfully begs me to not leave her side, even though my partner is waiting for me in our own bed. I feel I must promise to come back; I don't want her to cry. And later, as my male partner slept, I would slip back in bed with her for a while—*to make her happy.*

Two years later, I am in a pit of desperation, having ended yet another toxic relationship in Baltimore with "marriage #4." It's also after my fourth mugging in four months, in which a crowbar had split my scalp and scarred my skull. My studies at Johns Hopkins must stop. I decide to return to San Francisco, but I'll need a place to stay until I find a job there. I need support. I'm terribly broken down. Jessica is the only one I know who *might* just give me that....

Soon I'm forty years old and I've been living with Jessica for a year. She wants to have a rich lifestyle, so I got a high-paying job, a *terrible* job in a far-off jail with a three-hour commute. I rent a house in the lower upper-class part of the upper-upper-class Tiburon-Belvedere area. They say that Belvedere, a huge knoll in the Bay connected by a guarded strait to the Tiburon Peninsula, could sink under the weight of so much wealth. We've been invited to the yacht club; they do that to all newcomers, to "check them out."

Jessica spends her time finishing her dissertation and doing aerobics classes at a private gym where all the women are blonde and have strange breasts that do not move as they jump. Jessica doesn't need implants; she is naturally voluptuous.

"I have a theory about gays," she says. "There are two types of gay men. *Type A* gays are intrinsically, genetically homosexual," she pauses. "*Type B* gays have emotional issues due to abusive maternal bonding. They aren't *really* gay." Jessica stares lustfully at me, licking her lips. *"They can be converted."*

Jessica is constantly horny. She expects sex—actually, she *craves* sex nonstop. I've learned that if I close my eyes and visualize a man, I can ejaculate. She's begun lessons and "The Joy of Sex" is open on the bed at the appropriate page. Today, I must find the **G-SPOT** and she's getting impatient.

I fear my mother will slam the piano keyboard cover on my fingers.
"B-flat, MICHAEL, **B-FLAT***!"*

We're having a weekend getaway at the posh Sea Ranch, an alternative ultra-modern seaside community where I've rented a house. Jessica and I have taken the love drug, "Adam," or "Ecstasy." Being an alternative therapist in San Francisco, where *alternative* is mainstream, means taking Ecstasy from time to time these days. I've also drunk a bottle of wine.

We're sitting naked in the hot tub, looking at the ocean on a starlit, full-moon spring night. "So, Michael, what's your *ultimate* sexual fantasy?" Jessica asks.

I can't lie on Ecstasy; it's like a truth serum aphrodisiac. "I don't know…OK. How about a three-way arrangement with another man?" She doesn't like my answer, but I continue. "For instance, a bisexual guy, like Bill." I mention a tall, handsome black fellow who I've known and had sex with, and whom she's met.

"Sure, Michael. You're free to have that. I'd be fine with that. You could have sex with men, if I'm in bed, too. Or even, maybe on your own. Would you like to have children?"

A pause.

"I don't know…I think so," I reply hesitantly.

"You'd be a great father, you know. But I'm forty-four and time is running out for me. I saw my gynecologist and it appears I could still get pregnant."

Another pause.

She's convinced me that I'm "homosexual, type B" and now, "time's running out." Jessica is looking just like she did when she fell to her knees in the courtyard of the school—*imploringly.*

"Jessica, so, would *you* like to get married?" It's just a theoretical question, not a proposition. But people hear what they want to hear.

"OH, Michael! *REALLY?* It will make my mother so *proud!* She'll pay for the wedding and a honeymoon, too! We can invite…." Jessica is excitedly rattling off names of people to invite, and where to have the wedding, and how pricey is the diamond ring she's just seen at the jeweler's…

Ecstasy makes you do crazy things—it's a love drug. It's probably not a good idea to decide to get married while on Ecstasy. Jessica calls her mother in England. I call my parents and tell them the good news. My parents are surprised, but my mother seems distinctly happy. I want to make both our mothers happy. I tell my parents how much I love them. I love Jessica. I love everybody.

But I don't know if I love myself…

I've attended classes at the synagogue because there are things I must learn now. I've learned to say the wedding vows in Hebrew. We've rented an ultra-swank resort, the "Auberge de Soleil," nestled in the hills over Napa Valley for the special day. The wedding will be outdoors on one of the multi-level slate terraces overlooking the pristine vineyards below.

I'm sweating in my tuxedo under the hot summer sun. I'm wearing the now-familiar skullcap that hides the little, but growing, bald spot on my head. I'm finishing my fourth glass of wine. Bill, the bisexual guy, tells me to slow down. But I'm nervous, *very* nervous.

Jessica is floating merrily about like a helium-filled balloon. She chats gleefully with my soon-to-be English in-laws and the cluster of about one hundred of her "best friends." The entourage is a sundry assortment of upper-middle-class and lower-upper-class African Americans and English Jews. I feel uncomfortable about Jessica's *braggadocio,* how she boasts and commands audiences; it doesn't feel genuine and she likes the attention far too much. Now, she's showing off the twenty-thousand-dollar diamond engagement ring I bought her.

Her short, plump mother wants to know about my medical practice. "So, you're a doctor! I'm so *happy* you're a doctor!" The photographer has taken what seems to be thousands of pictures of our families, the crowd, and us; Jessica keeps asking for more photo shots of herself.

The Rabbi is ready now. The *Torah* is open on the pedestal table under the cloth canopy, the *chuppah*. Orthodox Rabbis will not officiate the marriage of a Jew and a non-Jew, but Jessica has found an alternative Rabbi. I think he's gay.

The wedding music starts…

"HUSH!"

I am standing next to Jessica under the *chuppah*.

My back is to the audience. My beautiful three-year-old niece is the flower girl and she's walking down the aisle tossing blooms left and right. The traditional ceremony begins: the wedding address, the benedictions, the sharing of the cup of wine. Then the *Ketuba* is read in Hebrew; the second cup of wine is offered to the bride and groom— *They can't possibly be "us!"*

I'm not in my body anymore. I gulp the sacred glass of wine straight down in front of the Rabbi and Jessica, who both frown at me. Then I recite the Hebrew words: *"Behold, thou art consecrated to me with this ring, according to the Law of Moses and Israel!"*

"MAZEL TOV!" I throw the empty glass furiously onto the slate ground and watch it shatter. 'It's too late to go back now,' I think.

We are taken to another table to sign the *Ketuba*. I'm not exactly sure *what* I'm signing in the book—the legal contract of a Jewish marriage. By habit, I sign "MD" after my name. Jessica scoffs, snatches back the Ketuba, and adds her PhD to get even. She says in an ominous *sotto voce*, "You have no idea what you've just signed, Michael. You're *mine* now!"

There are speeches and praises and toasts that I won't remember because I'm quite drunk. The elegant dining room has a central redwood post up to a cathedral ceiling.

The *Hora,* or traditional dance of celebration, begins during the elegant meal. Jessica and I are swirling around each other, holding the ends of a handkerchief, and then we are paraded around the room with applause.

I'm lying on the sofa in the flower-filled wedding suit after the ceremony.

"Michael, come to bed with me!" Jessica orders.

"No, I'm sorry, Jessica. I need to think."

I'm lying on the floor at home almost too hung-over to move.

"Michael! The plane leaves for Tahiti in two hours!" Jessica yells. I throw clothes into a suitcase haphazardly. I leave the rented tuxedo hanging in my closet.

Three weeks in paradise go by. Jessica spends most of her time crying and shouting at me. I'm reading French and getting drunk when I can.

One afternoon, I decide I want to see the interior of Moorea Island. I drive the rented Jeep in the heavy rain over a ravine, along four slippery wood planks that are barely wide enough for the wheels. A gushing swollen river thunders in the deep gulch beneath me. I proceed ahead into a non-traversable and impenetrable dead-end forest on the other side of the crevice. Soon, I'm jammed in by jungle on both sides and there's no way to go forward and no way to turn the Jeep around. It's virtually impossible to drive the long mile backwards in the pouring rain and with Jessica screaming at me.

Somehow I manage to reverse course, backwards across the rift and out of the dead-end forest.

We purchase a house in the up-scale Kensington Township, high up in the East Bay hills, and only a mile from my parent's home. Jessica complains, just as she complains constantly about almost everything. "The only thing I like about this place is the name, *Kensington,* because the return address looks good." Kensington is one of the wealthiest residential sectors of London.

By getting married, I also get to briefly enjoy the "normal" special treatment that heterosexuals take for granted and that I've never felt as a gay man. For the first time in my life, I can see how many doors open when you're straight and married. The opportunities and courtesies and favors are exponentially better than when you're gay. Unlike the impossible experience of freedom by changing to be white, I can test the truth of social conformity only this way—*by marriage.*

Nevertheless, it soon becomes impossible to deny my true sexuality; I occasionally revert to being actively, but not openly, gay again. After the wedding, Jessica retracts all that she said to entice me.

'It's OK to be gay, let's have children' now becomes: "There will be *serious* consequences if you insist on having sex with men, *MICHAEL!*" And, "I'd *never* have a child with you! You'd be a horrible father, *MICHAEL!*"

Jessica becomes dramatically furious, surly, and desperate. She reveals a self-absorbed and cruel nature that I'd seen many times, but now it's *constant.* During the O.J. Simpson trial, Jessica delights in threatening me. "Do you know how easy it would be for me to have you arrested now?"

One night when we are staying at my parents' vacation home at Lake Tahoe, she treats me with sullen coldness when I decline her demand for sex. I get so angry that I pick up a pointed Aztec stone carving and symbolically stab my abdomen near my groin. *I don't realize I'm acting hysterical and replicating a scene from my past—my naked mother and her knife.*

Jessica storms outside into the cold winter snow when I refuse to give her the keys to my car to drive away and leave me stranded. Scared by her histrionic behavior, I go outside to save her. I drive around to find her, and then I follow her, offering, pleading, "Please calm down and come back inside. I'm sorry. We can have sex now."

A police patrol car arrives. I explain that my wife is upset and I am trying to bring her home. He then interviews Jessica and returns with a squinted-eye warning. "Spousal abuse is a crime. She says you physically threatened her, but she'll give you another chance to cool it.

She won't press charges, but if she *does*, you're in jail!" The fact that I had not threatened her in the least, that she was angry because I wasn't sexually interested in her at the time, had no bearing on the prejudiced situation; the policeman did not ask my version of the events.

Jessica becomes consistently distrustful, dour, and cynical, as perhaps only the English have mastered. She deliberately chooses different sleeping and eating times; she refuses to help me in any domestic chores and insists I hire a housekeeper.

Jessica acts spoiled and used to getting her way, demanding to be in charge and in control of all others and all events. She stays theatrically angry and resentful, pouting and petulant. She diminishes my decisions and judgments, and heaps derogatory insults upon me— "You're *immature*! You're *selfish!*"

Her jealousy peaks when I get phone calls, and she's suspicious of all my activities when she is not present. She becomes envious of my income and appearance, even my car. I find her kicking her own car, shouting, *"You're a piece of junk"*—if only by contrast to my SAAB.

Under the guise of needing to protect herself, she avidly seeks an audience of allies in her friends, family, and therapist, artfully turning them against me. Jessica loves to have an audience and diminish me in front of other people. She paints *me* as the aggressor, dominator, winner, and victimizer, and *herself* as the weak, dependent, powerless, and neglected one. She threatens to expose me and scornful admonitions abound, especially in front of invited guests: "There are consequences for being gay that you'll *pay* for!"

With even *more* drama, she invokes an ominous future: "My witch relatives have *cast a curse* on you, Michael!" Then she adds, "I'm going to write a book about women who are abused by their gay husbands. In fact, I think I can make a *fortune* in the market! I'll start support groups and do a national lecture series... How would you like to be famous *that way*, MICHAEL?" Then her *coup de grâce*: "And now, because of you, *I hate blacks too, MICHAEL!*"

Tantrums and threats besiege me. I can't keep the façade anymore. I can't pretend to be straight. But the ending never quite ended. There were curtain calls and encores and flowers and rotten eggs until...

The eleventh hour, the eleventh month of marriage, one month short of formal requirements for filing for divorce, and I'm in my first rehab. Perhaps drinking my way out of the marriage saved me. It gave me time away from Jessica, to pull myself out of a terrible mistake, and it gave me an excuse to file for annulment.

Jessica then hated me as in a Greek tragedy.

She wanted *financial* compensation. I gave her everything I could: the house, the money. I assumed her debts and filed bankruptcy for myself. She wanted *emotional* compensation. She wanted redemption from the utter embarrassment she'd suffered in her family. But she acted *more* than disgraced; she wanted *more* than revenge. She'd come to rehab family counseling sessions and be told she was grossly inappropriate by the therapist.

She couldn't stop screaming, **"I WANT YOUR BLOOD!"** Hysterics, drama, contortions: I refused to be in Macbeth any longer.

I haven't heard from Jessica for eleven years now. She has an Internet ad for her therapy practice: "I specialize in supporting gays, lesbians, and other alternative lifestyles." I guess I gave her a calling: "Ex-wife, compassionate and supportive partner, of a closeted gay man." It's good for her business.

My Jewish wedding day

This complex, multi-part memoir addresses my father's clandestine homosexuality and incestuous behaviors, my own process of coming out, and a medley of my parents' reactions to my being gay— especially my mother's hostility.

THE CLOSET

I am four years old. Cullen is alone with my father in a private room of his medical office on the first floor of the building where home is the third floor. The door to the room has been locked for some time, so I wait on the back porch to talk to my father.

Cullen is my father's handyman. He lives in the *second*-floor apartment with his wife, Margie, who is my father's receptionist and nurse. Finally, Cullen emerges and comes to the porch to smoke a cigarette. He is shirtless, slightly sweaty, and *beautiful*. I'm in awe of his biceps and rippled abdomen, his trim, muscular torso, and his smooth ebony-colored skin.

A confused and foreign sentiment stirs in my five-year-old body. It's like on those long summertime trips to visit grandparents and relatives in the South. I'm falling asleep on the front bench seat of the car. My head is pulled down to rest on my mother's lap, and then pulled onto my father's, as if vying for my contact.

And the two laps are distinctly different.

*

My father decides to teach me golf when I reach early adolescence. It's *his* favorite sport and one where he can impress me with his skills. He buys me a kid's-sized golf club set and insists that I start to practice. It's irrelevant that I don't like golf, or that none of my friends play golf, or that softball or football coaching would have suited me much better.

And there is something very intimate in the first stage of practice from which I never graduate…

Dad says he must teach me how to hold the club and practice swinging it over and over. His body is plastered over my backside, his head pressed against mine as he whispers instructions in my ear. His hands slowly push my fingers into the correct position, even though I know it by heart. His arms are over my arms and his strong hands cover my hands. His torso and pelvis, his head and hands, never release their contact for the full practice session.

I feel acutely uncomfortable as I breathe in the air that he exhales. Any effort to free myself from his body, which is fused tight to the contour of mine, leads to an increasingly tight embrace and grasp. *I cannot escape.* And I can't concentrate with my father squeezing me so close as I lift my arms and execute the swing—the ball hooks sharply to the right, never straight. I finally push Dad off me and ask permission to end the training. Dad just shrugs his shoulders at his son's failure to enjoy his game and the day comes when he leaves me alone.

*

There is only one game I like that Dad also likes: ping-pong. I painted the green table an orange color to make it blend in with the 1960 decor of the finished basement, which had been designed for "the two boys" to have friends over and host parties that never happened. They'd even thought of putting bowling alleys in the basement. There was plenty of room.

The table separates Dad and me and I feel at ease because I can use it as my boundary. When my father competes with me, it's not for fun. He *must* win every game and show off his skill, just as he did when he and my mother had Bridge parties with neighbors at our home. Dad must always win, chortling in front of the demoralized guests.

He has never coached me how to play ping-pong. Like almost everything else in my life, I had to learn how to play on my own. Whenever I lose a volley, my father gloats, "I *told* you that you couldn't beat me!"

By the time I reach late adolescence, I can play Ping-pong very well. Dad challenges me to a game. By now, I know that my father needs the orphan's adolescent prize of being recognized as unique, and I am used to gratifying his ego. And I've grown to resent it. A rage seethes within me as the game starts. I know that my father sees me as a rival. His competitiveness precludes giving encouragement. Instead, he sends the message that I must always perform less than him so that his fragile self-esteem is not threatened.

But my serves have a lethal speed, a low-rising curveball to the extreme edge of the table. My backhand returns are quite good, too. The rounds are a dizzying and ferocious *SLAM* and *SLAM BACK*. My father begins to sweat as I win the first match. He is shaking with adrenaline and his grimace is as serious as a soldier in life-or-death combat.

Dad taunts me with what is another familiar refrain: "I bet you can't do it again!" He insists on a second match. He's *got* to win. I cannot be allowed to be better than him.

As I, too, get angrier, my swings and serves begin to reflect my fury and exceed the margin of the table. Sometimes, I slam the ball right at my father's face or so far behind him that he must work hard to retrieve it from underneath furniture and shelving.

He eventually wins the third match and I don't care. He laughs and ribs me, showing a smug pleasure in my defeat, as he will show in *all* my life's failures because, by comparison, he feels superior: "I *told* you that you couldn't do it!"

*

Dad has called me twice to come outside to help him mow the lawn, but I am engrossed in the self-pleasure of a kid, new to the discovery of masturbation. Surely, I'll be done in a minute and then I'll help him. I procrastinate, rushing nervously to finish.

I miss the sound of the lawnmower's engine turning off.

Suddenly, Dad throws open my locked bedroom door.

"I called you *twice* to—" Then he stares fixedly at his twelve-year-old son lying naked with an erection on the bed in front of him. His eyes are filled with intense and building passion for an eternal still-life *flash*. Finally, he blurts out, "When you've finished, come out to the backyard. I want to talk to you." He slams the door shut.

I am horribly frightened and ashamed, not by my masturbating but by my father's odd reaction. I throw on my clothes and rush to the backyard where Dad is hitting golf balls with a tense frenzy.

"Come here, *closer*," he orders. He leans on his golf club iron and tells me a story. "I know this doctor, an anesthesiologist, who can't stop masturbating. He's addicted to doing it compulsively a dozen times a day. He can't work because he even does it in the middle of surgery. You'd better be careful, or you'll end up like him."

Dad resumes hitting the golf balls as I walk back to my bedroom in shocked slow motion. There, I hide, "sleeping like an angel," until dinnertime. My shame gradually turns into rage, as I flash back on how Dad stared at me, how he hit the golf balls, and his fable that seems contrived and irrelevant to my need for reassurance.

By tomorrow, Dad will deny with absolute conviction that any of this ever happened. Within fifty years, I will come to realize that Dad was "the anesthesiologist" and he was telling me about himself.

*

It's my second year at Exeter and I've flown home to Erie for Christmas break. In my heavy fake-fur coat is an ounce of hashish concealed in the lining through a little hole in the right pocket. I have written in my diary about being stoned, taking LSD and other hallucinogens, and being so high that I was scared. My diary is mixed with matching binders of class notes locked in a suitcase.

The day after my arrival, my father calls me into the laundry room, far from my mother who is resting in her bedroom at the opposite wing of the house. I stand a few feet in front of my father who is looking down at something that he is holding hidden in his cupped hands.

"Michael. Your good mother found a hole in your coat pocket. She will sew it for you. Then she found something wrapped in aluminum foil, which she unwrapped. She thought it was chocolate and felt sorry for you for being so hungry that you must take chocolate around. *I've read your diary,*" Dad says solemnly.

My father then opens his hands to show me the hashish. He lifts his head up and I see tears falling down his face. I have never seen my father cry before.

"I'm going to have to punish you, Michael." Dad has *never* physically punished my brother or me.

"Just *how* do you plan to do that, Dad? Give the hash back to me!"

Dad pushes me and wrestles me to the floor. I fight back and we're equally strong now. Tears become laughter at the absurdity of the attempted punishment. Suddenly he relaxes all his muscles and lets his full body weight just lie on top of me, with his head next to mine for a long time.

Too long…

He sighs and then he holds me in a tight embrace, lifting his head to gaze lovingly into my eyes—face-to-face. His lips are close to mine, *too* close…

The look on his face is the same as when he caught me masturbating and massaging my mother. I shove him off and go to my room.

*

She pauses and seems to choke on the next sentence. "Then, the man went to the toilet and…your father went inside with him. They were in there for a long time. Your father said he had to do some sort of medical exam. Michael, I'm frightened…"

*

I'm twenty-one and it's my first trip home after coming out to my parents on the phone. My mother comments on how big my penis is…

"It would make a woman very happy," she exclaims.

I snap back, "It would make a man even *happier!*"

Is it hard for my mother to accept that I am cheating on her?

Then she gets angry and insulting. "So, how do you find homosexuals? I can smell *your* body odor. Is that the clue? You can sniff and smell their armpits for B.O.?" My mother notices that my lips are slightly chapped and she vilifies me more, "Your lips look like an over-used vagina!" I've tended to have a problem with chapped lips since I was a kid who tried to make his lips look thin.

*

My father takes me down to the basement to talk in total privacy in the ping-pong room. He tells me that he'd had a job as a bellhop in a fancy, segregated hotel in Richmond, Virginia when he was about my age. Homosexual men frequented the hotel. They paid my father to whip them with a wet towel as they masturbated. He tells me, "Because they were white, I hit them *especially* hard." He slams a ping-pong ball furiously into the air.

Then my father begins to approach me. I back into a dimly lit corner, thinking at first that his head is coming so close to mine to check my eyes, perhaps to see if I were stoned. Instead, I recognize the same expression I've seen so many times before. I am petrified by my father's look and energy.

It's not menacing, but…

This time the look is unmistakably sexual as his lips press onto mine and his wet tongue tries to penetrate the barrier of my closed mouth. I shove him backwards in horror and disgust.

"But Michael, I thought you'd *prefer* to just keep it in the family!" He's truly surprised at my rejection of his attempted incestuous advance.

The next day, Dad is driving toward downtown Erie and I am in the passenger seat. I avert his intense razor-sharp gaze on me by looking down, or out my side window with bleary, unfocused vision. He can hardly drive the car, for he is so distracted by having to stare at me.

Suddenly he yells, *"I see you looking at that good-looking man!"* I have no idea to whom he's referring.

"You're *looking* at him, *aren't you?"* I feel my father's incensed jealousy. I realize that Dad had to have been looking at the attractive pedestrian, not I. I was just staring at empty space, feeling acutely uncomfortable about my father's intimidating scrutiny. It would take the next thirty years to teach my parents to respect my boundaries.

*

My father begins to confide more to me when I'm married to Jessica, as if now he trusts that I'll harbor his secrets faithfully since we're in the same boat. But I have always been my father's confidant and secret-bearer. He always made me promise to never tell anybody, and I've always obeyed his injunctions. When I was less than ten years old, he told me that I have a half-sister, allegedly from a tryst when he was "just sixteen." He's been supporting her financially. She lives in New York City. *Period.*

That's all I'll know about a woman whose name is omitted, and who I will never meet. "Don't ever, *ever* tell your mother—not even after I die," Dad warns me.

"Why, Dad?" The reason was clear with no need for an answer: She would leave him or she would kill herself.

Once, when I am married to Jessica, Dad calls me at work. He begins crying as he recounts an encounter he's just had on a Caribbean cruise. My mother attended a concert in Panama City, off the ship, and he stayed aboard to visit a man in another berth. "Do you think I'll get AIDS?" He could barely speak through his sobbing. "I couldn't live with the thought of infecting your mother!"

I try to console and reassure my father, but he's nearly hysterical. Then I tell him that I don't ever want to hear any more about his infidelities and peccadilloes.

But my father's guilt is overflowing from the clandestine chamber of accumulated secrets spanning sixty years, and he *must* relieve the pressure. Remorse and shame about the past is killing him. And, now he can't use me to atone because I won't harbor his secrets anymore.

He decides to test my mother by telling her about his daughter's secret existence. "She won't mind," he says hopefully. "It happened when I was a kid, *before* we were married." Dad braces himself for his wife's reaction; if Mom is forgiving *maybe* he can tell her a bit more.

My mother is aghast and then furious. "If he kept such an important fact a secret from me, *for over forty years...*." Her wailing mixes gushing ire with lament. "I wonder what *else* he's not told me, what *else* he may have lied about!"

A fragile trust is ruptured as my mother instantly rents a different house and prepares for marital separation and divorce. Nothing will stop her, except... Dad's prostate biopsy shows cancer the next week. My mother is torn and tormented, "How could I leave a dying man?"

She relents and purchases not a separate house, but a new two-bedroom *third* home for both my father and herself, on the grounds of an assisted living community where Dad can die peacefully under her care and medical supervision. Now, she will have *three* houses that she doesn't like: the large, private house on top of the Berkeley hills where she'd hoped to grow old beside my father; another house at Lake Tahoe where she'd hoped to bring the family happily together for vacations; and the third, reserved for "ever-imminent" death. All three houses are on golf courses, to make my father happy.

And my father will never reveal anything else to his wife, even when radiation therapy and chemotherapy cure his cancer and he will enjoy good health for several decades with no terminal end in sight. In rare irony, the threat of cancer saved his marital life.

*

It has been proved that the only thing that addicts or alcoholics have in common is deceitfulness: hiding the truth of their habits in fear of judgment or reprisals.

Dad is jealous of my partners and tries to get too close to them. "So, how much does Jorge charge for sex?" he asks about my "ex" of six months earlier. He likes it when I date older men. "Well, if I weren't your father, I hope you'd want to have sex with *me*, despite my age!"

Dad asks for "good porn sites" on the Internet, "Just for a golfer friend of mine...." He tells me he's had sex with his patients, but "just blow jobs". He adds, "And that's not *really* sex." My last trip to a gay bar in my hometown of Erie leads to strangers grinning at my last name. "Oh, my, my... I know your father *quite* well."

One Christmas, Dad is very angry with me and I have no clue why. He's sitting with my mother beside him in the living room of their house in the hills. Suddenly he blurts out, "*You* can have all the sex you want, and I *can't!* Do you know how that makes me feel?" My mother looks out the bay window, perhaps at the Golden Gate Bridge, in a faraway daze. It's clear that she is blocked from hearing the words her husband has just spoken. At this point, she *must* stay in ignorance and denial.

I cannot sit next to my own father without his touching me. He places his hand on my thigh and squeezes it as I sit in the passenger seat of his two-seater Mercedes. I must have a partner or a friend whenever I visit my parents, for I am terrified to visit them alone. I need both a *witness* and a *protector*. That's one of the main reasons that I rushed into new relationships, *any* relationship, for many years.

Dad scares me when he approaches. When I am fifty years old, I send my parents a book on "boundaries" since my verbal protests are to no avail. I call to ask them about their reaction. They say that the book is a form of "elder abuse." My father is blunt. "As your father, I believe I have the right to touch you, *whenever* and *wherever I like*, if I'm not groping your genitals in public!"

My mother is also on the phone and I ask her if she agrees with my father. "Well, yes. *I DO!*" She affirms without hesitation, *without thinking?* I don't believe she's heard the meaning of his words. She just wants to feel free to give me hugs, and that's all this is about. I don't think she heard what my father has just said at all.

Then I did not speak with my parents for two years. Finally, they got the message—or so I thought. It was scarcely a year ago when my father cornered me alone again, in the family room of the Berkeley Hills home. He begins the same approach with the same look. I hold out my palms signaling 'STOP' and exhort, "Boundaries, Dad! *Boundaries!*"

He smirks and replies, "Just *try* to stop me!" Suddenly I become weak, frozen, and helpless in toxic shame. My father grasps my vacant exoskeleton in a desperate embrace, sighing heavily, almost crying, with his head on my shoulder. My effort to maintain my boundaries has failed yet again.

"I *told* you that you couldn't do it!" Dad whispers.

The following excerpt is somewhat tragic and depicts the life of a person with Cerebral Palsy and a medically disturbed brain,

leading to violence and an Obsessive-Compulsive Personality Disorder.

ORDERLY

My 6ᵗʰ marriage…

I decide to try another way to find a good partner—at a structured dating workshop called "Men Meeting Men." The bell rings every ten minutes for the chat with the next potential mate, and my score is zero for five attempts. The sixth and last fellow is slightly shorter and younger than me and he seems nervous. In some strange way, he reminds me of a quail.

He has closely cropped dirty-blonde hair with a streak of white dyed into a longer tuft sticking up in the front. He also has a tremor, a slight and barely perceptible shaking of his head when he speaks. His name is contrived, he says. He decided to overhaul his life history by choosing a new name when he finally came out of the closet a year ago.

Bill is the only one out of six who seems right. Not *exactly* right, but I'm devastated after my marriage and the events following the divorce from Jessica. I need somebody to resonate with; I must have love and I'm willing to take chances, even if it means betting on a lame horse.

Bill is not *entirely* lame; his abnormal gait is due to a congenital defect. He has Cerebral Palsy. Bill has an older sister and three younger brothers, and only he ended up with Cerebral Palsy. Eight surgeries and metal braces have resulted in his left leg being semi-paralyzed, two inches shorter than the right, and atrophied down to the size of a skinny stick. But in long pants, the deformity is generally unnoticeable; it's like somebody walking on a healing sprained ankle.

He begins to cry as he tells me what it felt like to be paraded in front of the Shriner's in an auditorium filled with other crippled children, so that he could be rated by the viewers like a breed of cows or pigs. Depending on how much pity *he* received, his *mother* received a yearly sum of money that she desperately needed to feed her five children.

Bill was raised Roman Catholic, which was perhaps unfortunate because his mother waited until after her five children were grown to get a divorce from a severely abusive batterer. He grew up near the beach in southern California and dreamed of being a surfer. He'd spend days at the beach watching the graceful elegance of the surfers and imagine that he could stand on the board, riding a wave, too. He'd listen to The Beach Boys on his transistor radio. Then, he listened to Soul music and his father took his radio and smashed it on the floor…

"I don't want to hear no *nigger* music!" He shouted.

Bill is thirty-nine now, and he's never had a live-together relationship. He has interpersonal issues. I am waiting for Bill in a bar on Castro Street, the gay Mecca of San Francisco. He arrives late, complaining about the public transportation. I want to finish my drink and then we'll go out for dinner. Bill is tense and protests that he has hypoglycemia, and it is now a whole hour after his routine dinnertime.

When we leave the bar, he bursts into a rage, shouting that I am inconsiderate of his needs. Then, he shoves me off the curb into on-coming traffic. I can't calm him down. By the end of the block, I cancel the date. I'm shocked by his violent behavior.

Bill calls me the next day. He is crying lamentably, and his sobbing is mixed with apologies and promises, "I'll understand if you never want to see me again. I'm so, *so* sorry. I don't know what happened. It may be related to my Cerebral Palsy."

The mere thought of rejecting a helpless victim seduces my compassionate heart. 'Perhaps I'm being too hasty and judgmental,' I ruminate.

Bill comes to my apartment for dinner. Unfortunately, he arrives early and I have another guy in my bed, who insists that he's in love with me and won't leave. Bill is not happy, watching my black trick emerge from my bedroom. Now, *I* apologize profusely. Once again, I can't calm him down, but I finally persuade him to stay for dinner—*on time*, this time.

Then we go to the indoor pool and sports complex; that's when I see him in swimming trunks and feel overwhelmed with sorrow and pity. I want to take care of Bill, maybe just for the night. He stays overnight and cuddles me in his horniness and in his well-developed torso, his muscular arms, and slender rippled abdomen.

Bill's father has just died in Kenya. After the divorce, he traveled there as an engineer and, oddly enough, he fell in love with an African woman. Bill saw him just before his death, the only one among his siblings to go to Kenya to see him—the only one who showed him compassion instead of hatred. Bill has a selective capacity for compassion, because he knows what it feels like to be rejected and alone.

I follow in the lineage of needing compassion from Bill. When I lose a bad job a few months later, I need both love and a cheap place to live. I urge Bill to let me stay with him for a while, and he reluctantly agrees; sometimes, in hard financial times and in lonely desperation, "finding a place to live" means "engaging a bad relationship." Sometimes, being crippled and growing up in poverty leaves a mark equal to that of being abused or black.

Bill has issues about order and orderliness. But he also has a warped brain. Bill has a junior college degree in accounting and works long, tedious days in a small placement agency where the owner is his only friend outside of his family of origin. He always stays many extra hours late when it comes time to do the payroll; every penny must be correct or payroll would be delayed. His job demands rigid perfection.

I alternate between *living in* and *fleeing from* his tiny apartment for the next year. It is crammed and cluttered with heaps of "things": piles of bits of paper and receipts, odd junk without any value, and crates and boxes without labels completely fill the physical space of the one-bedroom apartment. Two birdcages stuffed with twelve little birds and an incessantly screeching parrot with deformed claws produce a deafening, maddening intrusion of sound. And everything must stay *exactly* as it is, every day, without any changes whatsoever.

Bill demands *perfect disorder*. When he comes home, he is always suspicious that something might have changed or been moved, and he'd immediately search for the transgression; somehow, he'd "find" my betrayal of his orderliness. Perhaps a cupboard door is not completely shut or the closet door is not exactly one inch open on the right. Or perhaps the bed is not made correctly. Invariably, he would find a reason to rage and shower me with insults and accusations.

And everything inside his head must stay *exactly* as it is, too. Bill has just developed seizures; at unpredictable moments of emotional excess, his entire right side contracts into rigidity—a sort of transient spastic hemiplegia. He's had a brain scan and asked his doctor what it showed. The neurologist tried to reassure Bill, but admitted that the damage was very extensive. "The human brain is truly remarkable," the neurologist said. "It is still capable of functioning despite having what *looks* like a train wreck. Don't worry!"

The seizures involve the temporal lobe region, and that type of lesion is very tricky. It can lead to bizarre changes in personality and even mystical experiences. It can also lead to paranoia and aggressive rages. So, I feel even *more* compassion because I am a doctor and Bill is a victim and he is *almost* my patient. He suffers from a compulsive need to represent his derailed brain in the maintenance of environmental sameness. In a bizarre way, the chaotic packrat orderliness inside his home almost precisely reflects his brain's structure. His desperate need to control the external world reflects a terrifying loss of control inside his head. I don't realize, however, that my desperate need to rescue him from his suffering reflects empathy to the absurd extreme of martyrdom.

I *think:* 'I love Bill.' He was emotionally abused as a child. He's just come out and this is his first relationship. I *believe:* 'I can save him from shame and teach him how to love me.'

His pouting and rages occur daily. They are always followed with tears and apologies. Strict obedience to his beliefs and expectations is mandatory; it's "my way or the highway" about all ideas and all things. "How can I *win* here? You're not letting me *WIN!*" he screams when I try to engage a benign intellectual discussion.

His few clothes and belongings were procured with miserly angst. Above all things, Bill cherishes his one ultimate dream purchase—a red Cadillac. The car must be personally washed twice a week, in a detailed order of sequential steps. It must be kept spotless, forever "new," with a perfect chassis, frame, and shell. When I am ordered to help wash the car, he supervises every motion I make and closely inspects the result with diligence. When it is dented in an accident, he loses all self-control and a furious vendetta against the pathetic, elderly diabetic driver at fault lasts half a year.

Nothing ever moves, nothing ever changes, and nothing is ever learned. I *fixate:* 'I'm a healer. Bill is sick. He's a victim. He can't help abusing me.' I arrange for Bill to see an expert on anger, and then a good therapist at my own expense. He only goes to therapy a few times, saying in miserliness and looking at his glass jar piggy bank, "It's a waste of money." But he does learn to leave post-it notes all around the apartment, stating: "WHAT I WANT."

One day, a mutual acquaintance, who has known him for a few years, tries to broach the subject of non-violent communication. He recoils into sullen rage at the concept; for him, the only right way to get things done is to get angry.

I will spend many months living in motels and camping in tents away from Bill, and reach a crossroads of compassion without limits. But his concept of a relationship will never expand beyond a financial agreement, an investment not in love but in material security.

Under the mistaken belief that the interpersonal problems are due to living in such a cramped space, I will make money that enables Bill to buy *his* first house, and *our* first house together. He reasons that he'd get a lower interest rate as a first-time buyer; therefore, the house is left entirely in his name. I create a beautiful indoors milieu inside the new house, a haven for him to heal *his* internal space. But I will be unappreciated and badly mistreated in the process. I still must submit to exactly his way of doing things, from how to wash a dish to how to pull up a weed.

When I buy a pair of shoes, I'm frightened that Bill might notice—and he does. "You bought new shoes *without* asking my permission!" he roars. He throws a lit cigarette in my face and shoves me off the curb again.

"Come here. Tell me how you're going to vote on the ballot issues," he orders. There is a one-vote difference on a minor issue about Native American casinos. "You're canceling my vote! How dare you, *you asshole!*"

Another rage: He's throwing things, breaking glass, and shaking his head wildly. He dials the police to have them arrest me and take me away as an intruder, since the house is legally "all his." I snatch the phone from him. "Now you've crossed the line! *You've assaulted me!*" Bill screams.

Shortly after, I develop an acute episode of chest pain. Fearing a heart attack, I wake Bill up and ask him to please drive me to the emergency room. He storms around the bedroom, incensed, and then he strikes my chest with his fist, screaming, "It's always all about *you*, isn't it? What about *me*, huh? What about *me!*" Bill proceeds to have a seizure that lasts over ten minutes.

My nerves are on "High Alert" now. I must be careful; this is a pattern of escalation that will likely turn into greater violence. A tirade soon after gives me a clear choice and breaches my ocean of tolerance and compassion. "I want you out of here in one week!" Bill yells.

"OK. But with all my furniture and having to look for a place to stay, I can be out in *two* weeks. Would that be all right with you?" I reply. He's shocked that I might follow through and leave him, but his pride will not allow him to retract the order. By now, I'm sleeping on the living room sofa with a stick under the cushion, just in case.

'His brain is deteriorating rapidly,' I think in medical terms. 'He has an Obsessive-Compulsive Personality Disorder due to Organic Brain Syndrome and he could become *psychotic* now. I've got to get out of here quickly.'

And thus, I was soon gone, but the rages continued for a long time afterwards. Bill called the leasing office of the apartment complex I applied to, screaming that I was worthless and they'd better not rent to me.

His boss' husband was a lawyer and Bill convinced him to write threatening letters to extract "indebted money" from me, which I paid without contesting. My tires were slashed in the unsecured parking lot of my apartment building.

One day, I reminisced about my years with Bill.

I realized that he had never said the words, "You're right."

The last image I have of Bill was a chance encounter at a gym we'd both joined. "You're looking pretty buffed, Michael," Bill says with admiration.

"Thanks. I'm working on it," I reply.

"No, I think you've *got* it. *Your* body is perfect."

He turns and walks away with the familiar, twisted-ankle limping gait—*only worse.*

This relationship memoir describes the plight of a twenty-three-year old illegal Mexican immigrant, enslaved and traumatized upon arrival in America. The mosaic of both religious fervor and sexual compulsion is not unknown among the clergy. My partner's deep-seated racism and exploitation is kept hidden until the end.

THE MONK

My 7th marriage…

My 7th relationship begins a couple of months after the 6th ended. I've decided to try *another* partner search strategy: I will look for someone who is on a deep spiritual path. Clearly, such a person would share my values and be emotionally sound. Buddhism appeals to me.

I'm attending my first meeting of the Gay Men's Buddhist Fellowship in San Francisco. The group is comprised of about sixty guys and most of them are articulate and intelligent, and I'm feeling comfortable with them. I'm also feeling sexy; I've been working out for two years and my physique can't be more perfect. I'm wearing a tight tank top, just to flaunt my chest and biceps.

There is a young man who has caught my eye. It's the first time he's attended the Gay Men's Buddhist Sangha, too. He has a heavy Spanish accent, so I start to chat with him in my fluent Spanish to impress and maybe befriend him after the meeting. At first, he lurches backwards at my touch and then rudely ignores me. 'Maybe speaking Spanish insults his competency in English,' I fear. But his initial squint-eyed look and his recoiling denote…

Jorge is twenty-three years old. I am forty-six years old—exactly twice his age. He's been in the USA for only six months. He was a practicing Buddhist monk in Mexico City for the past three years, a *celibate* monk for that span of time. I'm shocked that such a young man would choose celibacy and I'm intrigued. Is he a virgin?

Jorge has a youthful sort of "acceptable" Narcissism. He likes to debate and argue about Buddhist philosophy and he is gifted enough to hold his own in English. It's cute; he thinks he knows everything about Buddhism and that he's always right. A touch of zealotry becomes his youth.

He lives in a rented room in a house far out in the suburbs, whose owner is an elderly gay man. It's actually more or less on my way home, too. I offer to give him a ride and he accepts with obvious leeriness. I can feel his horny energy in the car, and when we pull up at his house I take a chance and ask him, "Or would you prefer to spend the night with me, Jorge?"

He's a "virtual virgin" having had sex only three times and bursting with pent-up energy like only a youngster can muster. He immediately clings to me and we meditate together, sleep together, and I fall in love. But I tell myself, "CAUTION! He's inexperienced and very young. He will need to explore his sexuality! He won't stay *forever*, Michael." I know the risk but I can't resist it. I try to talk myself out of the madness. Besides, his story is so tragic that I want to help him.

Jorge is from Oaxaca, the mostly indigenous Aztec region of Mexico, with strange customs and foods. His mother is native Mexican mixed with Chinese. He is in the middle of eight brothers. His father is of direct Spanish lineage, and was once the editor of a leftist newspaper that supported the Mexican-Indian rebellion a couple of years ago. The government smashed his printing equipment and banned him from work. Poverty struck and the boys scrambled anywhere and everywhere— "survival of the fittest."

Jorge is very smart but he has dyslexia; he'd have no chance at getting a white-collar job in Mexico. So, he decided to first try to live in humble poverty as a monk. Then a "sort-of" relative, an adopted sister of his mother who'd separated from the family many decades ago, invited him to cross the border and work for her husband in northern California, in a sanctuary city called *Concord.* All he had to do was arrive there. With barely enough money, loaned to him by a true aunt, he tried to cross the border to freedom.

A ravine and a river…

A raft crowded with hopefuls…

Then scramble and *RUN FOR YOUR LIVES*…over the barbed wire fence and into the desert beyond. Twice, the Border Patrol helicopters snared him. Twice, jail and deportation, and then he'd try the third and last time; his money was nearly gone.

Sometimes violence cancels out violence and a door opens. A vigilante group of ranchers began to fire at the raft and the Border Patrol engaged the vigilantes. The diversion provided the few extra minutes needed to penetrate the desert and hide in the dense scrub.

Evade the helicopters and find water immediately to keep the elderly and pregnant alive in the desert…

Betrayed for ransom and run from a dank hotel whose owner turned them all in….

Find the bridge where the ruthless coyotes will take him north….

Extortions for everything of value and all the money left over at gunpoint….

Be deadly quiet, locked in the back of a windowless van…

Finally, Jorge is dropped off on a curbside in downtown Los Angeles.

Freedom!

A bus takes Jorge to Concord, California at last. The estranged evil aunt welcomes him into her group of another dozen fools. She has enticed, lured, and ensnared Jorge and many others into a well-crafted trap. All of them will know slavery in America.

Perhaps, it was the *trauma*…

Work or be beaten, maybe shot. Nobody would know—*they aren't even here*. Night-times, Jorge is locked in a garage, disoriented in a foreign land and without maps. Day-times, he is loaded, blindfolded, onto the van with tinted windows and taken to a worksite to paint buildings or carry heavy loads or dig in the earth. He is never given any money for his hard labor.

After several months of enslavement, Jorge escapes and runs away. He gets a house-painting job with three American low-lifers and learns to speak crude English: "SPANK THAT ASS!" they catcall women.

Perhaps, it was the *culture shock*…

Jorge is slowly learning about the mores of his new country. Fortunately, Jorge does not have to live on the streets; the Rainbow Community Center for Gays and Lesbians arranges for him to live in the house of an elderly gay man. And that's when I meet him.

Jorge is eager to move far away from the place where he lived in constant dread of being found, captured, and re-enslaved. We soon move to a little house in the scenic wine country of beautiful Sonoma Valley. There, Jorge's disciplined loyalty and dependency begins to clash with his adolescent defiance and independence. He becomes both my lover *and* my son for the next two years.

As my son, Jorge regresses to tantrums, always *wanting* something: A new CD by Madonna or more new clothes or just money, *NOW!* He must see U2 and the only tickets left for the group's tour are in San Diego, *NOW!* Or he'd kill himself. He cries after each daily tantrum.

He is amazed by America and he wants his material dreams fulfilled, even as he laments the deepening loss of his spiritual path. He longs for his family, whom he calls, then cries with guilt and nostalgia. "Why not tell them you're gay and you have a stable relationship with a doctor, Jorge? That way you'll have less shame and they'll not worry about you so much," I suggest. But Jorge balks and squints his eyes.

Jorge is passive aggressive; he offers to help cook and clean, but then forgets. He's afraid to explore the town outside our home on his own and I must accompany him everywhere. He has full-blown post-traumatic stress disorder. If a helicopter flies over our property, Jorge becomes petrified; he dashes off the porch and cringes underneath the bed inside. He is understandably afraid of capture and deportation again, so he stays alone in our lovely country cottage all day, while I go to my office to see patients.

Perhaps, it was the *boredom*...

Posing nude in the full-length mirror, he asks me, "Do I look fuckable?" Soon I had to sit down and stare in shock at the phone bills—the Internet porn sites and 900 calls. "Jorge, aren't you satisfied with me?" I ask. When I talk about my past sexual relationships, he gets angry and pouts. "It's like feasting in front of a starving man," he complains.

He refuses manual labor because he doesn't want his skin to tan dark like "the other Mexicans" —being light-complexioned means a lot to him. Besides, he's *better* than all the darker ones; his father is a Spaniard and he has a blonde brother who looks totally *gringo.* I set him up with carpentry jobs and non-field labor, but he refuses to go. Finally, I send him off to an excellent massage school for a residential two-week crash course, under a superb teacher who'd previously taught me and who I highly respect.

Suddenly Jorge changes.

He has a secret plan...

He wants something more…

He needs something that I can't deliver. Pendulums of extremes swing like a political backlash, and Jorge's celibacy is transfigured into promiscuity. I take him to gay men's retreats and he locks himself in the room, ashamed to come outside. "I'm too *ugly!*" he wails pitifully.

Maybe it's true. He has a congenital defect of his jaw, which protrudes and causes an unseemly underbite. But his beautiful brown eyes or, when he smiles, the bouncing energy of his countenance, his exuberant aura and enthusiasm, his soft slightly swarthy skin…

I love every part of him and I am obsessed with him.

Perhaps, it was his *envy*…

"Look at you! You have a perfect small mouth! You have rippled abdominals! You look like you're *twenty*." And that was possibly true. I felt like a kid again; being in a relationship with someone half your age can be rejuvenating. The rock concerts, the compliments, even getting carded along with Jorge at gay bars on the Russian River: All seemed to bring back my own youthfulness.

I start chatting with another couple at a weekend gay men's retreat. Then, just being curious, or maybe to make a point about my worthiness, I ask one of the guys, "Who do you think is younger? Jorge or me?" The new acquaintance ponders the question as he looks at Jorge's anxious face and then at mine. He finally says, "Well, I think *you* are, Michael." Jorge flies into a fit.

Perhaps, he just needed to *experiment*…

Jorge asks me to approach men at the retreat on his behalf, and tell a guy that he'd like to have sex with him. I do not want to do this, but my codependency has become fully active. I want to make Jorge happy. I approach the designated fellow and I say the words, "My partner would like to have sex with you. Would that be OK?"

The man misunderstands and thinks that *I* want sex with him, to which he eagerly agrees. Slowly, the correct request sinks in. "You mean *you* want me to have sex with *your* partner?" It's too awkward to proceed. But soon, I start to arrange three-ways to satisfy Jorge, but hating every minute of them.

Perhaps, he just needed to *individuate*…

Jorge becomes massively paranoid, depressed, and treacherous. He begins to lie and steal money. His tantrums get worse. He throws lit cigarettes in my face, just as Bill had. Then, he makes a call to somebody who he says is a friend in LA; he needs to go there immediately to find suitable work, which he says he cannot find living with me.

I wave goodbye as the Greyhound bus departs, and my heart and soul splinter, not knowing if he'd come back. I become so grief-stricken that I can't work and I lie in bed for a week. I call Jorge every day. After two months, he begs to come back.

He's afraid he might have AIDS. He never worked in LA. He lied to me in every phone call. He lived by means of his body in every gay bar, every night, and still needs more. With a warm embrace and crocodile tears, he promises to "not play around anymore." A week later, I come home and find Jorge in bed with an eighteen-year-old kid. Angry, betrayed, yet trying to not be jealous, I insert myself into the bed and start to play with the youth, to pull him away from Jorge.

Jorge insists on talking privately with me. "He doesn't *want* to be with you! You're too *OLD*." Then, with the original squinted-eye look from the first moment of our meeting, he adds, "And you're *BLACK*. That's why I never came out to my parents about you. If you were white, they'd approve of my being gay." How could I have missed all the signs of his ageism and racism?

Suddenly enraged at me, Jorge shouts, *"SO, GO AWAY AND LEAVE US TWO ALONE!"*

I finally realize that Jorge was looking for both sex and for a rich white Sugar Daddy to replace me during his stay in Los Angeles. Fury overwhelms me. Jorge is a lying, racist traitor. I get drunk and lambast Jorge in vitriolic Spanish until he cries.

I tell the teenage boy he must leave; he chooses to go to the Russian River where he has a place to stay with an older gentleman. He's a runaway from his own home. Jorge sits sullen and quiet beside me on the drive back home after dropping the stranger off.

I *SNAP*.

"PUTO! PUTO DE RENOMBRE! YOU'RE A FUCKING WHORE!"

"TE ODIO! I HATE YOU!"

I slap him repeatedly and hard and my car swerves across the road. His terrified wailings and apologies fall upon my deaf ears. He opens his car door and tries to jump out of the moving vehicle, and I yank him back inside. I've never struck anybody before.

I am suddenly in 9th grade.
Mrs. Butler puts on her white gloves.
She slaps me down to my knees.

Jorge steals my laptop and massage table and moves to a medium-sized city nearby. There he becomes a prostitute. He's been a prostitute doing sexual massage for the past seven years now. He doesn't know what else to do with his life. Jorge says that his path of spiritual service is through the offering of sex.

Perhaps, he's just an insecure kid trying to grow up, with low self-esteem and a fragile narcissistic shell.

Perhaps, without a Green Card, prostitution is all he can do in America.

Perhaps, he's a sex addict.

A few weeks later, I am lying alone in my queen-sized bed, grieving and insomniac. For some reason, I've been staring at the ceiling every night, ever since Jorge left. Suddenly I hear a shattering crack like an earthquake and I think that perhaps someone has thrown a rock at my window. I flash back to my childhood and wait to see a burning cross with bated breath. Then a four-by-eight-foot section of the ceiling of my large bedroom smashes down to the floor to my right. Then, another section falls to my left.

Within a minute, the vault of decomposed insulation material, dead rats and ravens, crashes down with a shower of hundreds of rusty nails and heavy chunks of beams and plaster, leaving a three-foot deep layer of debris. The entire ceiling has fallen all around a "cut-out" of my exact figure lying on the middle of the bed, and every possible inch of the room is filled with death outside my protected shell. If Jorge had been in bed with me, he would have been seriously injured or perhaps killed.

A voice whispers, "All will be revealed and resolved in time, Michael." I sense the presence of an ethereal being, whether Shiva or an angel or other entity, I do not know. But in that instant, I forgive Jorge for everything and am grateful for the sign of salvation from the invisible messenger that has freed me from my captivity.

This relationship memoir is quite sad and complex. In fact, I cannot describe it without getting choked up. It may evoke powerful reactions to all who may read it. Yet I cannot omit mention of the AIDS epidemic that decimated my cohorts.

PLAGUED

My 8ᵗʰ marriage…

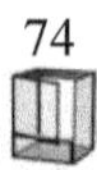

I don't like gay bathhouses and I've gone there only a few times in my life. They reduce a human being to a mere speechless body with only one function. But I decide to go to one after seeing a play in Berkeley. I'm forty-nine, and once again single and lonely. I'm not looking for sex and bathhouses are only about sex, but I haven't tried to meet somebody there before. I've tried just about every other way to meet guys and struck out. What could be the danger of just checking out one bathhouse?

I prudishly change into my gym clothes, but leave my shirt off, and start to exercise in the small gym inside. Guys notice me as they walk by, but don't linger because I'm partially dressed. Then, one fellow starts to workout beside me and he has a different energy that I like.

Santiago is *Afro-Cuban* American. He could easily be considered just black, but he's proud of his father who grew up in Cuba. He is slender, muscular, and dark-skinned. He is truly beautiful. We converse, then we connect sexually, and then we exchange phone numbers. Within a few months, Santiago is spending long weekends with me at my house in the countryside of Sonoma Valley.

Santiago is on disability for chronic depression.

He's been depressed for a long time, but it seriously got to him a year ago after a volatile relationship with a fellow who was addicted to methamphetamine. Santiago is poor and has had no college education. He works as a DJ and a freelance photographer to earn just enough to supplement his disability income and survive. He's got no money to share the costs of living together—he can barely scrounge up enough gas money to drive up to see me on the weekends.

He lives in a low-rent housing complex for the disabled, located in the downtown ghetto of the rundown heart of Oakland. Santiago grew up in a ghetto and knows its ways.

The mutual sexual appeal is unbelievable. His rippled body and nearly zero-percent body fat, his soft ebony skin, his deep voice and masculine demeanor, and his full lips that kiss me all night are indescribably perfect. I ask him if he's HIV-negative, and he says he was last tested two years ago and was negative then. He's had only one sexual partner over the past two years.

I've seen too many people, including most of my closest friends, struck down by AIDS; fifty percent of the gay community in my generation perished. I don't want to take the risk of getting infected. Somehow, I've got to protect my sexual boundaries more than those who've had a different upbringing.

Soon Santiago and I are in love with each other. It's our Saturday home movie night and I've rented "Angels in America" to watch together. The film evokes overwhelming emotions for almost all gay men; it depicts the indiscriminate effect of the early AIDS epidemic in graphic and unforgettable images and narratives. One of the couples in the production breaks up due to AIDS. A character is so frightened by his partner's declining health that he chickens out of the relationship, and then suffers horrible guilt.

After watching the movie, Santiago and I are on my back porch looking at the endless swathe of fields, pastures, and mountain ranges; it's a perfect California landscape in the last rays of evening sunshine. I feel strangely compelled to tell Santiago, "If you ever got AIDS, I wouldn't be the bad guy in the movie who abandoned his partner. I'd stay with you, Santiago."

But the movie disturbed both of us.

Without telling Santiago, I decide to get re-tested for HIV, just to be sure, just to assure my beloved that we are completely safe. The day I get my "negative" result, which always brings a wave of tremendous relief after waiting in infernal fear, I call Santiago. "I have good news, Santiago! I'm HIV-*negative*, so for sure I'm not infected and I'm safe!"

There is a silent pause.

I feel he's strangely distant and tense.

Finally, he replies, "What a coincidence. I just got my result today, too. I'm *infected*." He assumes that his last two-year relationship with the speed addict was what infected him.

That weekend I reassert my vow to stay with him, although, in tears, he said he would understand if I chose to leave. Yet there is a disquieting, heightened ambivalence in my mind. My principle attraction to Santiago is based on sexual chemistry. My primary pull *toward* him is now marred with a pull *away* from him. My source of enjoyment, rooted in feeling safe when I have sex with another, is now tainted with the fear of death, just enough to start to...

Santiago brings his cat, "Samantha," to stay with us at the ranch house for the weekend. The next morning, Santiago's cat is nowhere to be found. Santiago looks everywhere for Samantha, frantically searching for the pet he must have as his only fully trusted companion. Eventually, he collapses onto a chair on the deck sobbing, "She's off and running, *scared*."

I hold him and try to console him saying, "We'll find her. Don't give up, Santiago. She's still alive, somewhere. She'll come back." I sense that I'm talking about an abstract wish—something larger than the cat's return is *not* alive and *won't* come back. Samantha emerges from beneath the deck in response to Santiago's crying.

Santiago seems to love me, but he is becoming more hesitant to drive up and see me or to stay the whole weekend anymore. And he, too, becomes ambivalent, saying he's always been alone, he's never cohabitated, and he needs his private space.

I begin noticing that Santiago is generally quiet and self-absorbed. He spends hours mixing music in solitude, wearing soundproof earphones. He seems gloomy, pessimistic, and heavy, with deepening signs of being shut down by depression. Maybe that's understandable, given his bad news, or maybe he's been like that for years? I never see him smile or look happy. But maybe that's part of growing up in the ghetto and part of his sense of masculinity?

He's frustrated in his career and has never held a paying job. But that's because he's an artist. He rarely answers his phone, because the calls are mostly from creditors. He checks his bank balance daily and confirms yet another overdraft charge. He lives day by day, backed into the corner of poverty. He is not motivated to look for work, but not content to be poor. He has no vision or dream of the future. Perhaps that's his spiritual focus—to live only in the present?

A few months later, I'm facing tough financial times, too. I finally persuade Santiago to let me live virtually rent-free with him in the ghetto, in the home for the disabled. The bleak hallways and the demented shouts of cripples in wheelchairs is not a happy environment. The rundown neighborhood is crime infested and cars on the street are routinely broken into, stealing anything at all, even pulling out whole engines to sell for drugs.

Once we are living together in the tiny, cluttered one-bedroom space, Santiago withdraws inside himself to somewhere I cannot reach. Although we sleep together, he has stopped being affectionate and he turns away with his back toward me. His silence is broken with occasional sex, but it feels mechanical and lacking the original passion. I desperately want him to hold me, to support me, but he can't; he can barely support himself.

He seems to take forever to make decisions, as he ruminates and worries about the pros and the cons. I ask him to make a little room for me in his closet, which is crammed with haphazardly piled heaps of sundry, unused things, or to make some space in the bathroom for my toiletries. But he balks and procrastinates, as if it would entail too much work.

I rationalize that I am an intrusion into his space and I must accept second-class accommodations. But I do not feel like I'm living with a partner; I feel that Santiago wants to be here all by himself, unperturbed and alone, depressed for the rest of his undirected life.

I ask him to videotape a workshop on shame I am putting together. I buy Santiago whatever he says he needs for the job: video cameras, special recording equipment, then elaborate editing and splicing tools. I spend thousands of dollars for equipment he will keep. Yet, again, he procrastinates and no sound recording or video is ever produced for the waiting participants. 'He learned to be passive-aggressive to cope with his controlling mother,' I reason.

His mood is increasingly irritable, grumpy, but not very threatening; there's always somebody to complain about, especially his divorced, single mother. He has avoided intimate relationships with men and hangs out with female friends because of issues about self-worth. In mutual and opposing directions, he criticizes both himself and others, in cycles without exits.

Santiago lives in the past, in remorse and guilt about his life's mistakes and missed opportunities. He is so much like my depressed mother that I cannot stop trying to help him and lift him up. As Santiago becomes more cocooned and taciturn, I, too, get very depressed, for I am fully enmeshed with him. Then, something happens that changes the layout of the playing field of romantic love, a promise that I would break and a guilt that would plague me for a very long time…

Santiago begins to develop weeklong abdominal crises and multiple emergency room visits fail to reveal the cause. He starts losing weight; his face slowly becomes gaunt and unrecognizable. I realize that I must find somewhere else to live, *not* with Santiago, *not* in the housing for the dying. I pull myself together and rent a cottage, but I continue to see Santiago until he is at death's door.

He's finally diagnosed with a rare condition called "Splenic Artery Thrombosis," for which he must be on blood-thinners for the rest of his life. He begins to bleed easily, HIV-contaminated blood. Even kissing now becomes dangerous due to gingivitis. Sex is infinitely riskier; all I have is a condom-thin layer of protection against the teeming AIDS virus bursting in little spurts of blood, out of any orifice, *unpredictably*.

The last time I have sex with Santiago, he tells me, "I've finally decided, Michael…." He pauses, and then solemnly says, "You're the only person I've truly loved and the only one I could ever hope to love."

Santiago is admitted into the intensive care unit of a county hospital. His body wastes away to ninety pounds. While he is in the hospital, his mother suddenly dies. A week later, his stepmother dies. Santiago's depression deepens inexorably.

I break my promise to stay despite the risk of AIDS.

All he has now is Samantha, his cat, to comfort him. I am guilty of treason in love. I am the bad guy I didn't *want* to be, that I promised I'd *never* be, in "Angels in America."

I don't recall Santiago ever saying, "I'm happy."

This short, uplifting piece continues the subject of AIDS, but from a different perspective.

SPIRITUAL CONSCIOUSNESS

Arthur is brilliant and beautiful. He's been a fashion model, and then he chose to become an ordained priest. He lived with indigenous people in the mountains of Guatemala for three years, studying under the tutelage of a great shaman. There, he learned techniques that he now uses for himself.

Arthur is not sure how many years he's had AIDS; but, to the amazement of physicians, he can reverse a terminal state while in hospice, and make all the lesions of Kaposi's sarcoma disappear in three days of complete solitude, intense concentration, and deep rest.

Divine sleep in the Grecian temple of Asclepius…

Arthur has a light-hearted sense of humor and laughs at the thought of death, quoting Shakespeare, "Death be not proud! It is *I* that **YOU** should fear!"

I've fallen in love with Arthur.

I know he's a soulmate and a friend.

It's spiritual and platonic but…

One evening, when he gives me a crystal and silver amulet that he's made for me, I decide to ask to spend the night with him. Arthur is surprised, "Why can I *not* attract people? Even hideous and covered with disease, you are still in love with me!"

It's true that there are violaceous bumps on his face and nose, covering and disfiguring much of his visible body. Reluctantly, he allows me to stay the night. I hold and cradle his back and kiss his lesions—I know they aren't contagious. I don't care about the lesions of his body! I love his amazing soul.

Finally, one day, Arthur decides to surrender his body to his soul; his earthly experience and worldly lessons were finished. Arthur taught me that the meaning of life is to learn about the amazing healing powers and the indescribable beauty of *spiritual consciousness*. The miraculous, marvelous, and magical power of the spiritual mind trumps Death, itself.

Once again, the messenger frees me from my slavery, saying, "You learn from your heart, Michael."

The subject of Asperger's Disorder has recently taken center stage in psychology and psychotherapy, as well as attracting tremendous public attention.

To have a relationship with what may be analogous to a "human reptile," someone who is incapable of both empathy and reciprocity, is devastating to his or her domestic victims. The language used here replicates the flat emotional and abstruse cognitive world of such a person.

THE MAN WHO KNOWS NOT LOVE

My 9ᵗʰ marriage…

Without significant moments of love, I would not have survived my relationships. The truth is that each relationship contained experiences of intimacy, sex, or fun, which I interpreted as denoting "love," although they were sporadic, rare, and in contrast to the general pattern of abuse.

Perhaps, clinging to even abusive relationships provides these fleeting moments, like sips of water without food, to stay alive in the desert. Pure devotional and romantic love pulled me *into* passionate intimacy. And then, self-love briefly surfaced to rescue me and pull me *out* when the relationship ended. The illusion in shame-based relationships is "the appearance of love." The truth that engenders such relationships is always "the quest for love."

*

When I meet Guy, I am not exactly in my right mind. Once again, my self-esteem has been shot to near death, I'm very scared and I'm very lonely. It's my first day out of my second and last rehab, and an unforgettable, traumatic month of confinement.

It's probably *not* a good idea to select a life partner the day one leaves rehab.

In circumstances of demoralization, my codependent nature is at high tide and I tend to seek partners who are humble "lessers." Although it defies logic as an oxymoron and a mad paradox, I simply do not feel worthy of my own equals.

I've become aware that my heart is overcome by a desperate need for intimacy, which cascades like dominoes into dangerous behavior and false hopes. It starts with a dependent approach to a predator, along with a wish that the other will appreciate my gifts, bridge me into a peer group, bolster my boundaries versus my parents, and change into a loving equal. And right now, the need to be chaperoned into a peer group, to be protected from peer hostility, and to intimately bond with another has been grossly magnified by my ostracization during the rehab month.

So, why not find another fledgling strangler on the path of recovery?

Guy sits next to me in the AA meeting where we meet. He looks cute, even boyish, and he seems unusually shy or mellow like a hippie from the 60s. His knee pushes into mine, and I notice that his shoelaces are untied—rainbow-colored shoestrings and purple shoes covered with cat hair. He shares in the meeting, but I don't understand anything he says; the words are English, but empty and abstract. There is no message and no feeling.

After the meeting, we start making out in the parking lot like adolescents.

Guy seems eccentric and rambles a lot. He says he is Jewish and his mother is a psychotherapist, and he had just moved back to live with her after being thrown out by his wedded "ex," who was a spider man eunuch with arachnodactyly— who somehow got a woman pregnant that was just cohabitating with them for a Green Card, and Guy spent his last money to get the "ex" and the mistress legally married so they could keep the baby…

As I struggle to follow the twisted threads of disjointed events, I think, 'Poor guy! He's had a neurotic upbringing and he's deeply grieving. I'm sure this will pass.'

Guy speaks in a machine-gunned mumbled monotone, as soft and cadence-free as a pair of woolen stockings walking by themselves, drawing me ever closer to his lips to hear the words that are just audible at the farthest limits of my perception.

He says that the only other black man he'd had sex with, when he was eighteen, raped him, and that's why he's slow to warm up to me. He dropped out of high school and moved to Portland after the rape, where he's lived for the past twenty years. Guy says that our meeting is "God's will" and that I have been sent to heal him from the rapist. And, since I am a therapist with a good heart, I am also given to heal him from his abusive, controlling Jewish mother… ·

Right now, he's jobless and on General Assistance, which provides only a pittance as his sole income. He says that he'd worked in the sex industry before, and earned the title of "Chief Bitch" in charge of a gay whorehouse in Portland—his last, and only, long-term job of the previous two decades.

He'd had a janitorial job for a couple of weeks in a public storage facility, too, but the manager told him to clean a space from "top to bottom," and so he obediently started with washing the on top of the roof and worked on down to the basement, and then he was fired for *insubordination…*

He says he's never felt *happiness* and that he has chronic depression. Then, he takes a deep breath of air, breaching the concatenated puzzling stream of sentences, and says in the same tone of voice that he's never felt *love* and asks me, truly puzzled, "What *is* love? How do you know if you feel it?" I think he's either joking or engaging an abstract, theoretical debate…

Meanwhile, having initiated the relationship with Guy, I begin my "fixer-upper" routine. I devote my life to him. I call him to wake him up and to invite him for a morning ritual of coffee and bagels. I buy him helpful and increasingly more expensive gifts that will empower him and help him get his life back together. I want to assist him in finishing school, getting into a good career, and becoming self-sufficient.

Guy tells me that I can't ever visit him at his house because his neurotic mother refuses to let anyone come inside. Since dangerous homophobes live in *my* clean-and-sober house, I pay for precious getaways in hotels, resorts, or hot springs.

Like my mother, Guy is alternately seductive and kind, then hostile and cruel. Whenever we spend a block of private time together, Guy becomes instantly remote and then argumentative instead of intimate. When I try to work through whatever conflict has occurred, he becomes taciturn and I face a wall of absolute disinterest, a mute and dead silence. When I feel distraught, and withdraw to heal my wounds about the conflict, Guy suddenly tantalizes me with spontaneous little gestures: a piece of his jewelry, a deep kiss, a fleeting smile to indicate…*caring, perhaps?*

Later, I would know the truth: He is just a kid sharing his toys with his playmate and he is playing with my mind as his favorite toy.

Guy takes me into a diamond store and engages a salesperson to have me try on wedding bands. Then, he is astonishingly rude to the staff and boasts: "The owner of your chain is my *uncle*, so you'd better treat me especially well!" Nothing in the wedding band event is related to the marriage ceremony that I am imagining. Instead, by enticing the clerk and name-dropping, it is a pure instinct for dominance. When he tells me that the wedding bands were just for fun, he revels in my misery and mocks me in front of his friends, laughing about "how he'd fooled me."

In a brash move, I decide that the problem is just the strain of us living apart in hostile environments and it would be cost-effective to live together. I soon discover that living with Guy is like living with a mule. **NO**—*with a snake!* He is obstinate, unsupportive, ungrateful, and, over time, increasingly emotionally violent. It is unlike *anything* I've ever experienced in either my personal or professional life. After a brief honeymoon, I feel more demoralized than I've ever felt.

Guy quickly proceeds to give plausible reasons for his being strange. He is spaced out and unavailable because he has narcolepsy and sleep apnea, and his Ritalin hasn't kicked in yet. Yet, whenever he is around other people, he can suddenly perk up and even be effusively friendly and tactile. He doesn't do any housework because he has a rotator cuff injury, and can't push a vacuum or put dishes away. But he can lift heavy boxes of his toys and romp around on all fours with his cat at whim. He can't appreciate my cooking because he has reflux esophagitis. But he enjoys whatever his circle of playmates feeds him with apparent glee. He can't manage money or gain a livelihood because, he explains, "My overbearing Jewish mother traumatized me, manipulated me with her money, and over-pressured me to be successful."

I am slowly getting terribly nervous about Guy's ever more apparent strangeness; his hippie-style coolness is turning to coldness, his mellowness into aloofness.

He now tells me that he's been in many psychiatric hospitals, but he doesn't know exactly why. Guy makes recovery his top priority, even though he has no history of addiction or alcoholism at all. Our social life revolves entirely around AA meetings. His mother tells me, "I'd always prayed that he'd find *some cult* to belong to, *any cult*. AA will do just fine. Normal groups of people won't accept him."

Guy is inflexible and dictatorial. He is adamant that his routine AA meetings are the best, so I follow him there. He leads me up to a member who he knows will be the best sponsor for me, and I obey, *reluctantly*. The designated sponsor is an uneducated fellow I dated ten years earlier and I sense that he is now in a very dysfunctional relationship— *plus* he is twenty years my junior. But why not follow his advice? It will make Guy happy.

Guy takes on a "God Complex." He sincerely believes that he is gifted by his strangeness, and that God works through him. I begin to discover that he has an elaborate, twisted inner world, filled with delusions and frightening preoccupations revolving around violence, the macabre, and the paranormal. He manipulates the spiritual aspects of AA with astute cleverness, to the point of proving to me that *I am powerless over him, and that I must accept life with him as unmanageable.*

On the rare occasions when he sleeps in the bed, his back is turned toward me but sometimes he holds my arms so that they embrace his chest. In my reveries, he is demonstrating love. In the morning, I thank him for reciprocating my affection. "Wrong *again*, Michael," he snickers. "I was *cold* and you were *warm*." Generally, Guy sleeps on the living room floor, holding his cat in preference to sleeping in the bed with a human. The cat is *both* warm and soft.

As I sleep alone, Guy stays up until very late playing video games with an odd absorption. One night, about 3am, I go to see the game he is enthralled with; it's so violent that I freak. "That's *nothing*, Michael. You should see the other game I like better!" He grins with sadistic glee.

Guy is fascinated by the phenomenon of "spontaneous human combustion" and shows me Internet pictures of people who suddenly exploded. He wants, almost more than anything in life, to learn the power to do that. He is also obsessed with cars and had squandered his inheritance from wealthy grandparents on useless and discarded *real* cars, and collected thousands of *model* cars. And he knows everything about cars, down to the detail of how to build each engine.

Gradually, I resort to what I do best when I am threatened. I research, I think, I try to figure people out. I begin to look for a diagnosis that will make sense to me. At first, I choose a silly self-help book entitled, "How to Cope with Difficult People," and discuss my being a bit of the "super-agreeable" type and Guy being "the clam." He agrees, but remains completely silent and unresponsive.

"So, what?" he adds.

Then, I go to the ancient and mystical "Enneagram" system, and explain to Guy "I am an Enneagram Two—the pleaser. Maybe you're a Six—the devil's advocate?" He agrees that the Enneagram explains him very well, but refuses to change any of his negativistic behaviors.

"So, what?"

Then, I go to the psychiatric manual—the DSM-4. In the index are some "proposed diagnoses requiring more research." I explain the "Passive-Aggressive Personality Disorder" to him. He agrees that he meets all the criteria but, again:

"So?"

As is typical in cases of abuse, Guy convinces me that *I* am unreasonable, and that *I am abusing him* by expecting him to resonate or reciprocate emotional responses. What is *not* typical of abuse patterns is that Guy never budges from his conviction of being inculpable; he never shows contrition nor apologizes for his growing cruelty. His unflinching stance of emotional non-reactivity keeps me in a state of self-doubt. Eventually he reveals his true Self; Guy embodies a *reptilian* essence that gloats in the diabolical. He is not what society can call "human." My earnest search for love had finally configured my consummate karmic nemesis.

It is not until Guy, himself, begins announcing in meetings after our separation that he has "Asperger's Disorder" do I come to realize what is going on. I did not know that Guy had Asperger's. In fact, I'd never even *studied* the diagnosis, which had only recently drawn the full attention of the mental health field. It is a pervasive developmental disorder and part of the autistic spectrum.

Guy extracts a sadistic satisfaction in driving those who love him to the brink of a nervous breakdown and he is fully aware of this. Without the biological capacity for empathy, emotional resonance, or hypothetical thought—which are all parts of the diagnosis of Asperger's Disorder—he simply can't put himself in another's shoes and imagine how they feel. And he doesn't care how others feel. When he is informed that his behaviors hurt another person, he is totally complacent and even enjoys the fun.

Our last week together, Guy reveals his absence of love and core of aggressive hatred. He ruminates, "I wonder why I treat everybody else better than you?" Then, "I *know* I am noncompliant, noncommittal, and non-communicative." Next, "I have come to realize that *whenever* I sense that you want or need something from me, I can't help but to *refuse* to give it to you."

His parting words to me were both profoundly disturbing and helpful. "*You* should look at why you choose relationships with dysfunctional partners. And *I* should look at why I have to be the dagger that destroys everyone who loves me."

The noblest of human sentiments, empathy and love, do not exist in Guy. In the absence of empathy, *cruelty* manifests. In love's absence, *hatred* appears. Only the reptilian instinct for dominance and non-specific sexual expression remain intact. We barely lived together for three months, but it took me a year to come out of an emotional blackout of *psychobiological dysregulation*, in which I was kept tormented.

Guy has the literal power to warp another's brain; fortunately, he cannot cause spontaneous combustion. I had tried to emotionally resonate with someone who has a profound defect in the ability to perceive and to process human emotions. It's like sticking one's fingers into a high voltage electrical outlet and trying to establish rapport with the current.

What hurts me most about Guy is how he suddenly, mysteriously, and completely shut me out of existence. It was like a snake being uninterested and unfazed, witnessing its brother being hacked apart by a golf club. I have never experienced such cold hatred: *total erasure*. I guess I can't understand a human reptile.

His only words to me, knowing how I was suffering during the course and the ending of a major romantic commitment to him, were by email: "I'm sorry that you are in such misery, but your misery was created *for* you and *by* you."

I also realize that I will never be able to fully process what happened with Guy because it is too far away from the realm of reason. It also helps to realize that the intensity of my experience with Guy will probably never be repeated in my life, since only one in perhaps ten thousand people have Asperger's.

Not all who are afflicted turn out like Guy—he's just such an unlucky guy. I had loved an image that was only reciprocated in my imagination.

This pinnacle relationship memoir depicts the denial and self-sacrificial, or codependent, devotion of a father towards his identical twin adult sons that violently abuse him.

The language replicates the profanity in the sons' menacing style of extortionary control and reflects the increasing prevalence of the opposite of child abuse— "parental abuse."

DOUBLE TROUBLE

My 10ᵗʰ marriage…

Victor is currently my only trusted friend; therefore, he is my best friend. There is a special challenge involved in writing about my last relationship, which is still a legal domestic partnership. When a relationship is not frozen as an imprint of the past, when it continues to evolve and change in the present, a history of trauma transforms into forgiveness and even gratitude. But forgiveness is only conceptual at first, and it must manifest as deep *physiological* change for true healing to occur. That's one of the reasons that I must write about my last relationship.

The other reason is that I want to save my best friend from psychic death. Growth is life and, conversely, stasis is death. Fixed patterns indicate the demise of any living process including relationships, as well as the stagnation of the brain's creative capacity. It is the nature of the brain to change in response to one's environment. Conversely, trauma patterns are fixed like grand mal seizures; they are stuck, indelible abnormalities within the cerebral cortex. This book proves that trauma patterns can evolve into normalcy, with deliberate effort and under the correct circumstances.

Victor is growing in tandem with the creative adventure that is the birth of this book. Victor is the only person who is reading this book as it also evolves and changes. His critiques are valuable to me—except that he has no critiques. He only has enthusiastic praise and support for my work. If there existed one central issue when we were partners, before I ended the tumultuous three-year relationship several months ago, that issue would have been that Victor did not, or *could* not, truly listen to me. The miracle of the book is that now he knows me by means of written literature in a way that verbal communication could not achieve.

*

I've been trying to meet potential partners through the Internet, the classic dating sites, and I've discovered a few disheartening facts. First, virtually nobody is telling the truth, whether it is their true age *minus* ten years, true height *plus* four inches, or true intentions of seeking a sexual tryst, masquerading as looking for love.

I've also discovered the horrible extent to which racism persists in the gay community among my age group. My little bit of research has shown that a *non*-black gay man, over the age of forty and earning more than forty thousand dollars per year, is ninety percent likely to reject *any* black prospect.

"And I'm a member of the upper-upper class, by dint of race, genealogy, income...."

Nine months wasted by Internet profiling and I've just canceled my subscription to all services in dismay. Then, on the exact last day the matching service runs my posting, the *very* last moment, I get a response—as if it just crept through the crack of the closing door.

Victor and I meet and I instantly recognize him. I'd met him at a spiritual retreat four years earlier and I recall his intriguing mind and warm embrace. I'd always planned to phone him, but I'd lost his phone number.

Victor is a professor of sociology in the University of California system. He is also a criminologist and a published researcher who has everything going for him. He knows all there is to know about juvenile delinquency, having been a top-level administrator at the California Youth Authority for twenty-five years.

Victor comes from a hardworking Norwegian background and is now ten years out of the closet. He's ready to settle down. The long weekend together that immediately follows our first date convinces me that we are sexually compatible. So far, a good score: sex, mutual interests, great communication, ambition, initiative, and we both feel relaxed together.

What could go **wrong?**

Victor has two twenty-five-year old identical twin sons who are not quite **right**.

If there were a perfect partner for me, it would have been Victor. I will always love him, for he is truly a good man and a devoted father.

But I wonder, is he a *foolish* father?

He has hypertension, depression, and deafness for high-pitched vocal-range sounds like screaming. He has late onset attention-deficit disorder and can't focus anymore. Victor is burnt out and needs help. Codependency suggests extreme devotional attachment; burnout means obligatory *suspension* of excessive self-sacrifice. People who are burnt out just don't have any capacity left for the extremes of full codependency, such as martyrdom, engulfment, and enmeshment.

I am desperately lonely.

My self-esteem is very low after a year of Internet rejections.

I have no money, I'm about to declare bankruptcy, and I need a cheap place to live. *Déjà vu?* Once again, I engage in my most dangerous behavior: *dependent approach.* For now, Victor's twin sons are an abstraction, a matter that doesn't concern me. Besides, at zero out of nine in the last inning, I'm willing to take another gamble.

The moving day arrives.

Victor and a friend are helping me load the U-Haul truck at my old apartment. I will soon follow Victor to his home in the state Capitol, where I've never lived before, and set up residence in his lovely suburban house.

I have known Victor for only two weeks.

I'm about to move into his never-visited house.

I am about to meet his two twenty-five-year-old sons for the first time.

Victor is distracted by multiple phone calls as we pack; there's some sort of emergency with the son who lives with his ex-wife. But Victor is generally distracted; he needs detailed instructions on what to pack, when to take it to the truck, and where to sit until I ask him to move something else.

The score on "initiative" is dropping.

'Perhaps, he's distracted by his family emergency, or perhaps it's because of his ADD,' I wonder. Victor doesn't like to be told what to do; he just slows down and forgets. 'Perhaps he's passive-aggressive?' I dread the thought. I suppress an intuitive whisper, 'Perhaps it's a way to discharge anger when enmeshed with people who are overtly aggressive.'

I drive the U-Haul up to a large two-story lakeside house in a tidy Sacramento neighborhood. Victor prepares me to meet his son inside. "Remember, he's a bit slow to warm up to people. But don't worry, the two of you will get along just fine."

Beyond the front door is a sight that no civilized mortal should ever have to see. I am greeted at the door by a manic pitbull that jumps hysterically up to lick me. His son, Twin #1, is in a dead slumber and locked in his room upstairs.

Then, I look around to discover that the living space is *unlivable*. There is a near total devastation of the interior: ubiquitous broken glass, dirt, and filth are scattered throughout the house's gutted insides; countless cannonball-sized holes have been kicked through walls; doors have been ripped off their hinges and are missing; and broomsticks have been speared through the cabinetry.

Toilets have been stuffed and plugged with paper and glue; shaving cream and sticky debris has been sprayed or thrown up to coat the ceilings; and most furniture and appliances have been broken into pieces. And there are dozens of plastic bags piled halfway up to the rafters in the garage—all filled with brand-new clothes mixed with raw steak and rotting garbage to intentionally attract rats.

I spend the next six months repairing, rebuilding, fixing, cleaning, sanitizing, and resurrecting tens of thousands of dollars of wasted clothing and valuable furniture. I will also pay rent because Victor is heavily in debt. The more work I do, the more evident it is that Victor has been horribly abused for a very long time.

Every day for six months, I get up early and work as quietly as possible, because Twin #1 demands complete silence while he sleeps it off until the afternoon. Only *he* is allowed to produce noise, a constant, deafening noise. But in the morning, he sleeps overdosed and nodded-out, so that gives me a window of time to race around and repair the damage from the day before, and maybe make a bit of progress ahead of the backlogged damage. I slave furiously on my hands and knees, listening carefully for Twin #1's stirrings. I exist in a growing and dreadful fear, because when Twin #1 regains consciousness…

Victor's hope and secret desire is that I will relieve him of being a codependent caretaker for his sons. I commence the bridging, placating, serving, healing, curing, and salvaging of Twin #1. But soon, he'll blast the TV or blast me and go on a destructive rampage. Then, I lock myself in the bedroom and wear soundproof headphones to protect my eardrums from high-decibel, high-pitched noise.

The first morning after my move-in, Victor asks me to accompany him to a county psychiatric facility from which his other twin, Twin #2, is being discharged. He lives with his mother and he'd been arrested and put on a 5150—a psychiatric hold based on potential danger to self, others, or property. Apparently, he was harboring knives and other weapons and issuing verbal threats to kill his mother and her boyfriend. Victor's hope is that I will persuade Twin #2 to voluntarily agree to go and stay in a private psychiatric hospital nearby. Victor wants me, as a physician, to convince the young man to submit himself to longer treatment.

The county psychiatric ward is overcrowded as always. The masses of disturbed patients who arrive in daily streams have no beds to sleep on nowadays. The *really* nasty, belligerent sociopathic ones are just too dangerous to keep in the same space with the frail, geriatric schizophrenics. It's best to release them quickly for the safety of all others, including the staff. Especially if they threaten to sue and declare they have connections. The most highly abusive, manipulative and murderous types are released first, and then they usually end up in jail.

So, Twin #2 was signed off to go home or go away after one night's stay. He passed a mini-mental status exam: "Who are you? Where are you? What day is it?" The next question, required for psychiatric assessment, is routinely omitted: "Do you know *why* you are here?"

Twin #2 is a large and loud man. He is pacing and raging inside the lobby of the hospital. "What the *fuck* took you so long to get here, *Huh?*" He yells at Victor upon our arrival. I am instantly scared of this man whose behavior spells out the *initial* message: "Borderline schizoid who is not willing to take medications." As Victor requested, I suggest to the youth that he go, voluntarily, for medication and treatment review at a good hospital.

His wild response fully spells out the *second* message: violence.

Any sane observer would take the ensuing ranting of verbal threats, the menacing body language and demeanor, as quite serious. For, if not now, sooner or later, it is very plausible that such verbal threats will eventually proceed to physical assault.

And, soon he will...

"These two faggot TWINKS don't know nothing, but they'll see! Oh, yeah, they're going to fucking find out what's in store for them! Let them just wait and see. Their fag smiles won't be around for long. I can promise them that!" Hollers Twin #2, as he stomps around the nursing station in the hospital's lobby.

Victor says that the threats are just blustering; the boy would *never* hurt anybody. He's used to his sons' nearly daily threats of suicide and their threats to kill him or their mother or *anyone* close to their parents.

The staff in the lobby just shrug their shoulders.

Death threats, which the psychiatrist had determined weren't uttered to *him*, had just been assuredly uttered in public to *us*, but...

Too late. The discharge order has been signed and quite probably the staff is happy to get rid of the aggressive troublemaker.

Twin #2 refuses to get inside his father's car and storms off down the street, screaming. He is without shoes, but wearing jeans and long socks that hide the countless scars of self-inflicted lacerations on his legs and ankles. Soon, he will lose several quarts of blood from a slice that will bleed for two days and require over twenty staples—because he will explode, because he will not wait, in any "DAMN ER."

Slowly, Victor reveals the Twins' psychiatric histories.

Neither has lived independently with success.

Twin #2 was briefly placed in an apartment, only to be evicted after six months for demolishing its interior. Only Twin #2 has ever worked, as a stock clerk in the back of an appliance warehouse where no interpersonal skills are necessary. It's a specially arranged job, thanks to family connections—a job with an income that goes entirely toward buying drugs that he will lose in a year.

Skirmishes with the law occur bi-monthly and the Twins are used to being handcuffed and taken away for nights in a psych ward. But they have studied law and know how to argue and lie their way out, confident that Victor will rescue them and will never press charges. With the exception of drunk driving and my letters providing medical excuses for non-attendance at court-ordered work during probation, "So far, so good." The Twins have had nil experience with the criminal justice system, and they've been protected from jail because of Victor's political influence.

Neither twin has ever had a date, nor any interest in an intimate relationship. Certainly, no decent girl would tolerate such foul and aggressive behavior, anyway. Neither has ever had a real friend. Victor insists that they *do* have friends. One elementary school acquaintance comes over and gets high with them once in a while. An immigrant from Southeast Asia befriended Twin #1, to escape overcrowded poverty and live rent-free in Norman's house. Then he ran off petrified after one week.

There is also the dreaded professional burglar and thief who comes freely into the house. "Yeah, I'm good at it," the burglar boasts. "I see an open garage door and, well, I just can't help it. I've robbed over two hundred homes and I haven't been caught yet!" He laughs, takes another hit of weed and spits on the patio. Victor insists that he's polite; the burglar doesn't curse him or make homophobic insults.

Victor points out that the boys are really considerate of their pitbull; they put a dozen water and food bowls all through the house for him. To have *one* untrained pitbull with studded accessories on a long, *long* leash is good; but soon, *two* are better. It makes a nice impact on strangers when one of the twins walks the dogs after dark. But even the dogs throw themselves into my arms or hide under my bed when Twin #1 gets wild.

Of course, make the perpetual caretakers pick up the dog shit. *"Look at all that shit in the yard! You goddamn better pick it up, now, or I'll...."*

Victor has fully protected his sons from the inside of the judicial system.

He works in the system and knows the strategy. Both boys have been given every opportunity, including private schools for troubled youth where the rich and famous *opposites* of Exeter went to avoid juvenile hall. A few years earlier, they had been rushed outside of the USA to an expensive sanctuary in Mexico to escape detention. Invariably, they were kicked out of those places, too; the schools that specialize in recalcitrance deemed them *too* recalcitrant. But Victor justifies the expulsions, saying that the schools were corrupt or run by religious fanatics, and that his sons were being abused there.

Victor watches Twin #2 as the ER doctor injects anesthetic into the gaping wound from his mid-leg down to his ankle. The youth is screaming in high-pitched yelps and fighting the staff that tries to hold him down. "He's just always been super-sensitive to pain," Victor states. His son starts to gag and vomits on his father. Victor feels dizzy and walks to the waiting room where he loses consciousness and collapses on the floor.

"No way! I don't have any trauma from the boys. There is something wrong with any person who gets upset by their behavior!" Victor declares emphatically.

Twin #1 currently lives inside the house with Victor because his mother will not allow him to ever live with her again. He is prone to truly psychopathic behavior. At age twenty-five, he had refused to ever finish school past an arranged GED. He scoffs and refuses to work or to contribute in any way to the household. He also refuses to communicate without shouting and screaming profanities and insults at his father, and then at me. He is clever enough to routinely subject his father to threats of violence, blackmail, and extortion. The incessant cruelty works; he has learned how to force his father to give him whatever he wants.

"I want *new* clothes! You make me wear rags, FUCKING COCK-SUCKER, BOY BAIT! If you don't give it to me *now*, I will…."

The actions usually involve breaking, pawning, stealing, blackmailing…or *killing*. The threat is immediately enacted with violent behavior, such as kicking holes in the walls, ripping apart valuable furniture, and, of course, nonstop insults, shouted curses, and death threats. A precious object, *any* object within reach, is grabbed and smashed. Rip all the leaves off a houseplant, smash a phone against the wall, or kick the legs off an antique table.

Destroy *anything* on impulse!

The effect is dramatic. The violence will not stop until Victor surrenders and doles out money or rushes to a store to procure the desired object.

"I got to have a new computer! This one is a piece of shit, you *retard*, you son-of-a-bitch *asshole*!" screams Twin #1. Victor must appease his sons, so the "buying game" starts. The new computer is bought and then, without gratitude, there are more insults and derisions and screaming and violence, "It's not perfect!" Victor will exchange it, upgrade it, repair it, or buy accessories for it, *anything* to placate his poor son.

Next the "pawning game" starts. The new computer is pawned for drug money and Victor will pay to reacquire it, then it's pawned again and again; in six months, a single computer was pawned six times.

Then, the "stealing game" starts. Precious silver cutlery or troves of fine art, the house alarm system…

And all that money means a *lot* of drugs.

To have a shiny sixty-thousand-dollar, top-of-the-line sports car, or to have a new, menacing, big wheel pick-up truck, also means gas money to go get the drugs and transport them in the vehicle. Both twins live to get high, but Twin #1 *aspires* to become a heroin addict.

He has never known any other purpose in life.

He does not *experiment* with drugs, from nonstop marijuana to hefty overdoses of the most potent narcotics on the market. He's *researched* his drugs of choice in a layperson's PDR, with notations and tagged pages, to find those that appeal to him—with the hope of attaining absolute mortal oblivion.

There are nightly rituals of overdosing on one hundred sixty milligrams of crushed and snorted oxycontin, until he nods out. The maximum safe dose of oxycontin is sixty milligrams of slow-release formula per day. Every morning he vomits, retching in violent withdrawal. I watch him nearly lose an arm from arterial compression during the nod. I watch him lose weight and become dehydrated, until he is clearly at Death's door.

Victor has devoted most of his life and finite resources to help his sons: expensive new car money…gas money…drug money…wasted food money…discarded brand-new clothing money…repair the damage to property money…money gone up in smoke for no reason whatsoever…

And the two boys get all the money they want, until Victor is fending off creditors' hourly calls. Until Victor must give up the teaching career that he loves just to cash out on early retirement. Until Victor must default on his mortgage and lose his house…

And yet, Victor is *still* in debt, *still* driving an old, cheap car without air conditioning or maintenance, and *still* working post retirement. Soon, the twins will have their own homes; Victor will live homeless.

Victor is a good father who can't bear the thought of throwing his sons out onto the streets. He is convinced they could not survive there. He knows what would happen to them because he's worked twenty-five years for the California juvenile justice system.

And his sons know he'll never throw them out, too.

"Everything I ever loved has either been stolen or broken," Victor says with tears welling up in his eyes.

Victor will have the same tears as he cradles the image of his twins as newborns, holding his arms out and looking into his open palms, whispering, "You just don't understand what it's like, having held them in my arms as little babies."

The blinders of paternal denial in Victor become metal shutters welded shut. I must use plastic and rubber shutters—my soundproof headphones—that help protect me from the cursing and screaming that are specially rehearsed and timed for Victor's arrival home from work on weekdays, and constant over the weekends. The best time to get Daddy is when he's tired.

"They talk loud because they have a hearing problem," Victor rationalizes. "*Be quiet*, Michael! They're very sensitive to any noise!"

"They really have a low tolerance for pain," Victor justifies. "He needs to mutilate himself, it helps his pain."

"It's all their mother's fault. She has an unstable mood." Victor transfers blame, adding, "They just *think* about killing her."

"They talk foul like the TV characters 'Beavis and Butthead,'" Victor explains. "Don't you know *anything* about their generation?"

"*Victor!* Please listen!" I urge. "Your son is vomiting again. It's serious. He's in withdrawal."

"Oh, no, he's always had a sensitive tummy as a child. That's normal for the boy," Victor denies.

His son has narcotic-induced gastritis and a wasting syndrome.

"*Victor!* Please!" I beg. "Your son is transporting narcotics in his car and mixing with types who could kill him."

"Oh, no. He wouldn't do that. He just likes to say such things to impress people."

His son has told me the route and details of his drug trafficking.

"*Victor!* The threats to murder your ex-wife and her boyfriend have caused her to have a heart attack!"

"No way! My ex-wife is a hypochondriac. She doesn't have a heart problem." His ex-wife is admitted to the CCU for a massive triple coronary myocardial infarction due to stress.

It is a normal reaction to experience *panic* when violent abuse exists. It is also normal to experience *rage* when another denies the existence of violent abuse.

It's been six months since my arrival at Victor's home. Twin #1 faces death from narcotic abuse. A family conference with Victor, his ex-wife, her boyfriend, and myself is convened, at my insistence. I facilitate and an intervention is planned out. I will take his sports car away and together, as a family, we would stipulate that he could not have it back until doing a rehab program.

The next morning, Twin #1 sees me driving his car away from his upstairs bedroom window. He immediately goes on an unprecedented rampage of total mayhem and destruction in the house and yard. I try to brace the master bedroom door shut with furniture, letting the addict's dog cower under my bed. The doors are kicked down. Police come, yet once again, and they chastise the youth, and they also chastise Victor for *tolerating* such abuse.

"Don't give in, Victor. Get him outside help, *quickly*!" the policeman exhorts. Victor does not want to press charges, of course. When the police leave, the critical moment, the 'Truth or Dare' confrontation occurs. I muster the courage to walk up to Twin #1 who is ripping his room apart.

I stand in the frame of the doorway.

Before I can say a word, the young man's face is an inch from mine. He splutters, screaming, "My dealer is on his way here! He has a gun, *and he hates niggers!* HOW WOULD YOU FEEL WITH THE BARREL OF A PISTOL DOWN YOUR FAGGOT NIGGER THROAT?"

I surrender.

I pack my bags.

Victor relinquishes and returns the car to his son, saying he can't carry out the planned intervention without me. Nothing will change, except that the young man will eventually get into an expensive methadone maintenance program with no plans to ever get off narcotics.

After nine months apart, I try again.

I rent a *separate* house, located within ten minutes from the boys.

It's close enough for Victor to buzz over there when necessary. I think that, maybe, this will be enough to take him out of that hell and begin to think rationally again. Both twins are now living in Victor's house because his ex-wife's health could no longer bear the burden of Twin #2's drugs and violence. It is arranged so that neither twin will know where I live or where their father spends his nights.

The weekends are filled with Victor bringing carloads of hidden precious objects from his attic to store safely in our secret, shared house. Otherwise, I rarely see my partner. His sons' enraged calls and emergencies pull him away constantly. Besides, he still has to do the never-ending list of his own house's maintenance, up-keep and repairs.

The beautiful, suburban house will soon go into foreclosure, the house where the perpetual "boys" live for free, where they will not work, where they will only *make* work to be done.

He also has to bring his sons groceries and their take-out meals. In addition to Victor's shopping lists, they spend an extra eight hundred dollars a week on food. "They're picky eaters," Victor says.

After seven months, I move to the North Bay Area to take my last fulltime job as a doctor, and to try again. I harbor the hope that the *long* distance and *long* weekends away will break Victor's enslavement to his sons. But Victor's weekends away from his sons are virtually the same as if he were living in the house with them. His late arrivals and premature departures are predictably unpredictable. When present, he is absent, locked in worry and a vague, dissociated state of mind.

One cannot just take horrible, ongoing abuse without subconsciously discharging it, and thus becoming abusive, too. Victor has to vent his own pent-up, subconscious rage on *somebody*. It is disguised in the form of passive-aggressive behavior, such as constant teasing and scoffing when I express my emotions. He has lost the ability to validate the subjective experience of another, because he has repressed the totality of his own.

He has even lost the ability to give verbal reassurance.

He stammers and stutters and can barely utter the simple words I give him to repeat after me: "It must be *anguishing* for you, Michael."

One also develops a need to engulf somebody else, to compensate for the huge chunk of one's own Self that has vanished due to the abuse. One has to "play the victim" outside of the real abusive situation, since that role cannot be discharged safely in front of the abusers; sadists attack when another appears weak.

Abused persons are reluctant to seek professional help; the shutters of denial make therapy threatening, and the deep ocean of grief makes it terrifying. Victor scoffs at psychological work and the realm of psychology. "Doing psychological work will make *anyone* go crazy and become a hypochondriac. It's well known that *all* therapists are crazy. I suspect that most of them were crazy before entering the field," Victor pedantically asserts.

Moreover, he negates the need to do work on himself, saying he's already participated in a T-group in college and a weekend series of some program he calls "The Process" when he was first married, thirty-five years ago. I convince him to go to couples counseling with me, but the counselor bluntly states that it's a hopeless situation unless Victor places his sons in a supervised setting.

"I'm not so psychologically unsophisticated as you and the counselor think!" Victor sulks about the therapist's recommendation.

A person can only be as honest as they are willing to be aware of their true feelings. Victor has repressed his feelings deeply in order to survive in hell. One can only be as reliable as they can set limits on unpredictable outside interferences. One can only manifest self-sufficiency to the degree that they take the initiative or they have the guts to say "**NO**," and stop giving when the gift does not empower others toward their own self-sufficiency.

I do not believe that Victor really suffers from hypertension, chronic depression, Attention Deficit Disorder, or even deafness. One has to cope with chronic abusive challenges, *somehow*. The depletion of his neurotransmitters is completely understandable. His brain patterns are in double jeopardy, *double trouble*. The loss of resonance due to living with the disruptive neurosignatures of his two sons is not theoretical— *it's certain.*

Until he lets go of his sons and delegates them, according to their needs, to outside help, Victor will remain a victim of a level of abuse that is neurotoxic and lethal. Unacknowledged and untreated trauma, especially when it has reached the level of Post-Traumatic Stress Disorder, is extremely dangerous.

Victor is finally in therapy for codependency. He is hesitantly seeking the deeper work that is needed to address his major issue, which involves yet another form of neoslavery. It's the escalating and grave social issue of *parental* abuse.

Meanwhile, Twin #1 has been charged with a triple felony using firearms. Victor solicited my help as a physician to certify that the young man could not survive a prison environment, and it worked. Then, the young man became a skid row alcoholic…

Twin #2 lost his warehouse job due to escalating drug use.

Twin #1 will probably die from an overdose, and Twin #2 will probably be murdered by another druggie.

I'm afraid that my best friend, Victor, won't be able to grieve the loss.

MICHAEL HOLLOWAY KING

100

Michael King, MD is a graduate from both Harvard College and Harvard Medical School and he has had over four decades of experience in healthcare and communication skills. His love for biopersonality, consciousness, neuropsychiatry and international health prepared him to explore the essence of human nature.

He specialized in mind-body therapy in his alternative practice, and he has also worked in virtually all aspects of conventional medicine. He is currently a pioneer in social engineering and the first physician to address shame and social oppression, pinpoint their psychobiological roots, and invent treatment programs to resist them.

Dr. King is an expert in writing technology, listening skills, and public speaking, so writing a multi-genre, memoir-driven novel, "Hide and Play Dead," came as naturally as his self-help professional literature in "Overcoming Oppression."

Michael currently has a private practice in psychotherapy and psychiatry in Desert Hot Springs, California where he specializes in the treatment of shame, abuse, trauma, and social oppression.

His treatment process is based on high empathy, high rapport, client-centered approaches, along with somatic therapy and non-invasive emerging technologies in the neurosciences.

His current writing project is a study manual and workbook to accompany "Overcoming Oppression." A guide to his treatment system for healthcare professionals will soon follow—representing a paradigm shift for most of the social sciences and the field of medicine.

"It is time for the healer to emerge from the walls of clinical medicine and tackle the social milieu where illness is perpetuated. It is time for a new and revolutionary branch of medicine to take a stand against the primary source of human suffering in the world today."